Verona

Travel Guide

2024

Alex V. Keever

Use this QR code to get access to the map guide to Verona

Table of Contents

Introduction

The first time I visited Verona, I was immediately struck by its timeless beauty. Walking through the narrow, cobblestone streets of the historic center, I felt as though I had stepped back in time. The ancient buildings, adorned with colorful frescoes and intricate balconies, told stories of a rich and vibrant past. I remember standing in awe in front of the Arena di Verona, an ancient Roman amphitheater that has stood the test of time. Attending an opera there, under the Italian night sky, was a surreal experience that I will never forget.

One of my most cherished memories is visiting Juliet's house. As I stood on the famous balcony, I couldn't help but think of the countless love stories that have been inspired by Shakespeare's timeless tale. The walls of the courtyard were covered in love notes from visitors around the world, each one a testament to the universal language of love that Verona speaks so fluently.

Verona is more than its iconic landmarks; it's a city where every corner holds a secret waiting to be discovered. The bustling Piazza delle Erbe, with its lively markets and charming cafes, is a perfect example. Here, I enjoyed countless mornings sipping espresso, watching the city come to life. The blend of ancient history and modern vibrancy creates an atmosphere that is uniquely Veronese.

The culinary delights of Verona are a journey in themselves. I still remember my first taste of risotto all'Amarone, a rich and flavorful dish that perfectly encapsulates the region's wine heritage. Dining along the banks of the Adige River, with the gentle sound of water flowing by, is an experience that nourishes both the body and the soul.

Verona is a city that invites you to explore, to dream, and to fall in love. Whether you're a history enthusiast, a culinary explorer, or a romantic at heart, Verona offers something special for everyone. As you turn the pages of this guide, I hope to share with you the magic of Verona that captured my heart.

History of Verona

1. Roman Grandeur (1st century BC–5th century AD):

Our story begins over 2,000 years ago, when Verona blossomed as a Roman colony. Imagine a bustling city at the crossroads of important trade routes. Witness the construction of the magnificent arena, its tiered seating soon echoing with the roar of crowds during gladiatorial combats and chariot races. Stroll through the Roman Theater, a smaller amphitheater dedicated to theatrical performances, and picture toga-clad Romans enjoying comedies and tragedies. Verona became a strategic military stronghold, its importance was solidified by the construction of the Ponte Pietra, the city's oldest bridge, still standing strong across the Adige River.

2. Medieval Maneuvers (5th century AD–13th century AD):

Verona witnessed the rise and fall of various rulers, including the Ostrogoths and the Lombards. The city became a battleground for power, with fortifications being strengthened. One such example is Castelvecchio, a fortified castle built by the Scaliger family in the 14th century. This imposing structure, now housing the Castelvecchio Museum, stands as a testament to Verona's turbulent medieval past. Don't miss the nearby Scaliger

Tombs, the elaborate gothic funerary monuments of the Della Scala (Scaliger) family, who ruled Verona for over a century. These ornate structures, adorned with intricate carvings and heraldic symbols, offer a glimpse into the power and prestige of this once-dominant dynasty.

3. The Scaliger Dynasty (13th century AD–14th century AD):

This period marks a golden age for Verona. The Scaliger family, led by the charismatic Cangrande I della Scala, ushered in a period of stability and prosperity. Grand public works were undertaken, including the construction of the Castelvecchio bridge and the expansion of the city walls. Art and literature thrived under Scaliger patronage. It is believed that it was during this time, under the watchful eye of the Scaliger rulers, that the star-crossed lovers Romeo and Juliet met their tragic fate, immortalized by Shakespeare.

4. Venetian Rule and Beyond (15th century AD–present):

Verona's story continues with its annexation by the Venetian Republic in the 15th century. The city became a vital part of the Venetian empire, enjoying a period of relative peace and economic growth. Venetian architecture left its mark on Verona, with the construction of elegant palaces and the expansion of the city walls. Following the fall of the Venetian Republic, Verona passed through various hands, including Austrian rule and, finally, unification with the Kingdom of Italy in the 19th century.

Chapter 1: Getting Started

Planning Your Trip

1. Step 1: When to Visit Verona

• Spring (March–May): Pleasant weather with blooming gardens and fewer crowds.

• Summer (June–August): Bustling with activity, ideal for outdoor dining and catching an opera under the stars at the Arena. Be prepared for higher temperatures and tourist crowds.

• Fall (September-November): milder temperatures, vibrant fall foliage, and grape harvest season in the surrounding Valpolicella wine region.

• Winter (December–February): Fewer crowds, cozy cafes, and the magical Christmas markets (December only). Be prepared for colder weather.

2. Step 2: Accommodations

• Heart of Verona: Immerse yourself in the historic center by staying near Piazza delle Erbe or the Arena.

- Budget-Friendly Options: Look for hotels or guesthouses on the outskirts of the city, offering good value and easy access to public transportation.
- Unique Stays: Explore converted palaces or boutique hotels for a touch of luxury.

3. Step 3: Crafting Your Itinerary

- History Buffs: Dedicate a day to exploring the Roman Arena, Castelvecchio and its museum, the Scaliger Tombs, and the Roman Theater. Don't miss the Castel San Pietro for breathtaking city views.
- Romance Seekers: A must is Juliet's House with its famous balcony. Explore romantic sights like Ponte Pietra, the oldest bridge in Verona, and stroll hand-in-hand through the Giardino Giusti, a serene Renaissance garden.
- Foodies: Indulge in fresh pasta dishes, savor local cheeses and cured meats, and don't forget to sample a glass of Valpolicella wine. Take a cooking class or embark on a food tour to delve deeper into Veronese cuisine.

• Opera Enthusiasts: Plan your trip around the renowned Verona Arena Opera Festival held during the summer months.

4. Step 4: Beyond the City Walls

• Lake Garda: Take a day trip to this picturesque lake, a haven for water sports, charming towns, and breathtaking scenery.

• Mantova: Immerse yourself in Renaissance grandeur with a visit to Mantova, a city adorned with stunning palaces and art treasures.

• Valpolicella Wine Region: Explore rolling vineyards, sample the local Amarone wine, and indulge in delicious regional cuisine.

5. Step 5: Essential Tips

• Purchase a Verona Card: This pass grants free access to many attractions and discounts on others, along with free public transportation.

• Learn some basic Italian: A few key phrases will go a long way in enhancing your experience.

• Comfortable Shoes: Verona is best explored on foot, so pack comfortable walking shoes.

Savor the Local Cuisine: Don't be afraid to venture beyond tourist traps and try traditional Veronese dishes.

The Best Time to Visit

1. Spring's Gentle Overture (March–May)

Spring tiptoes into Verona, cloaking the city in a cloak of blossoming wisteria and vibrant tulips. The air hums with a gentle warmth, perfect for strolling along the Adige River or picnicking in the Giardino Giusti gardens. This is the season for leisurely exploration. The tourist hordes haven't descended yet, allowing you to truly savor the city's historic core without feeling jostled. Imagine wandering through the echoing halls of the Arena, bathed in the golden afternoon sun, or standing on Juliet's balcony, serenaded by the chirping of birds instead of camera clicks. Spring is also a haven for budget-conscious travelers, with lower accommodation rates and lighter crowds making it an ideal time to score a charming hotel tucked away in a cobbled alley.

2. Summer's Grand Opera (June–August)

The summer sun ignites Verona, transforming it into a vibrant stage. The heartbeat of the city pulsates with the rhythm of the world-renowned Arena Opera Festival. Imagine the thrill of witnessing a dramatic operatic performance under the starlit sky, the ancient stones of the arena amplifying the soaring voices. The city thrums with infectious energy. Cafes spill out onto piazzas, laughter floats through the air, and the aroma of freshly grilled food wafts from open trattorias. However, be prepared to share Verona's charm with a larger audience. Hotel prices climb, and popular attractions can get crowded. But if you don't mind the buzz and relish the opportunity to soak up the city's festive spirit, summer offers an unforgettable Verona experience.

3. Autumn's Golden Curtain Call (September–November)

As summer's heat wanes, autumn paints Verona in a breathtaking palette of golden hues. The crowds begin to thin, and a sense of tranquility descends upon the city. Imagine meandering through the streets carpeted with fallen leaves, the crisp air invigorating your senses. This is the season for indulging in the harvest bounty of the surrounding region. Imagine yourself sipping a glass of robust Valpolicella wine produced from grapes ripened under the summer sun while savoring a plate of freshly picked local mushrooms. Day trips to the nearby Lake Garda become particularly appealing, offering vibrant fall foliage reflected on the still water. Autumn offers a perfect balance: pleasant weather, fewer crowds, and a touch of melancholy beauty that resonates with the city's romantic spirit.

4. Winter's Intimate Soiree (December–February)

Winter transforms Verona into a wonderland of twinkling lights and festive cheer. The Christmas markets come alive, tempting you with local crafts, delectable treats, and the intoxicating scent of mulled wine. Imagine cozy evenings spent in charming cafes, sipping hot chocolate as snowflakes dance outside the window. While some attractions may have reduced hours, the city's historic core takes on a magical ambiance. The absence of crowds allows you to truly appreciate the grandeur of the arena and the intricate details of the Scaliger Tombs. Winter in Verona offers a unique opportunity to experience the city's quieter side, perfect for those seeking a more intimate and introspective travel experience.

Entry Requirements and Visas

1. Citizens of the European Union (EU), Iceland, Liechtenstein, Norway, and Switzerland:
Congratulations! As fellow Europeans, you enjoy the perks of freedom of movement within the Schengen Area. For stays less than 90 days in Italy, you simply need a valid passport or national ID card to enter Verona.

2. Citizens of Visa-Free Countries:
Several countries outside the EU enjoy visa-free entry to Italy for short stays. Check with your nearest Italian embassy or consulate to confirm if your country falls under this category. Typically, you'll need a valid passport with at least 6 months of validity remaining from your intended date of entry. Additionally, some countries may require proof of onward travel and sufficient financial resources for your stay.

3. Citizens of Countries Requiring a Visa:

If your country isn't visa-free, you'll need to obtain a visa before traveling to Verona. The reason for and length of your visit will determine what kind of visa you need. Below is a summary of the most popular visa classifications:

• Schengen Tourist Visa: Ideal for short stays for tourism purposes, up to 90 days within a 180-day period. Documents typically required include a completed visa application form, a valid passport, proof of accommodation, proof of sufficient financial means, and travel medical insurance.

• Long-Term Visa: For stays exceeding 90 days, perhaps for studies or work, you'll need to apply for a specific long-term visa type relevant to your purpose. The application process and required documents will vary depending on the visa category.

4. Applying for a Visa:

The visa application process is usually initiated at your nearest Italian embassy or consulate. It's recommended to start planning well in advance, as processing times can vary depending on your nationality and the workload of the embassy or consulate. Here are some helpful tips:

- Gather Required Documents: Ensure you have all the necessary documents as per the specific visa category you're applying for. Missing documents can lead to delays or even application rejection.

- Schedule an Appointment: Most embassies and consulates require appointments for visa applications. Plan ahead and book your slot well in advance, especially during peak travel seasons.

- Visa Fees: Be prepared to pay visa processing fees, which can vary depending on your nationality and visa type. These fees are typically non-refundable, even if your application is rejected.

5. Travel Insurance:

Travel medical insurance is highly recommended, even for short stays. Unexpected medical situations can arise, and insurance can provide financial coverage for medical treatment and emergency repatriation.

Health and Safety Tips

1. General Safety:

- Petty Theft: As with any tourist destination, be mindful of petty theft, especially in crowded areas like Piazza delle Erbe and public transportation. Keep your valuables secure, avoid carrying large sums of cash, and use a crossbody bag that zips closed.

- Pickpockets: Be particularly vigilant in crowded areas and on public transportation. Keep your wallet and phone in your front pocket or on a secure money belt.

- Scams: While uncommon, be wary of individuals offering unsolicited "help" or overly friendly locals trying to sell you overpriced souvenirs. Trust your gut instinct and politely decline if something feels off.

2. Sun Safety:

- Pack Sunscreen: Apply sunscreen with SPF 30 or higher liberally and reapply every two hours, especially after swimming or sweating.

- Hydration is essential. Always have a reusable water bottle with you.

- Seek Shade: During peak sun hours (typically 11 a.m. to 4 p.m.), seek shade under umbrellas, awnings, or trees.

• Sunglasses and Hat: Protect your eyes and head with a wide-brimmed hat and sunglasses that offer UVA and UVB protection.

3. Health Precautions:

• Vaccinations: While not mandatory, ensure you're up-to-date on routine vaccinations recommended for travel to Europe.

Medical Insurance: Travel medical insurance is highly recommended. It provides financial coverage for unexpected medical situations during your trip.

• Mosquitoes: Mosquitoes can be present, especially during the summer months. Consider using mosquito repellent, particularly in the evenings.

• Pharmacies: Several pharmacies (farmacies) are scattered throughout Verona. They stock basic medications and over-the-counter remedies.

4. Emergency Situations:

• Emergency Numbers: In case of emergencies, remember the following numbers:

• Police: 112

• Ambulance: 118

• Fire Department: 115

• Hospitals: Verona has several reputable hospitals. Ask your hotel staff for recommendations or research hospitals in advance in case of need.

5. Additional Tips:

• Comfortable Shoes: Verona is best explored on foot. Pack comfortable walking shoes with good traction, especially if you plan on exploring the historic center with its cobbled streets.

• Learn Basic Italian: A few key phrases in Italian can go a long way in case of emergencies or when communicating with locals.

• Respect Local Customs: Dress modestly when visiting churches and religious sites. Be mindful of noise levels in public areas, especially during the evenings.

Chapter 2: Travel Essentials

Packing Tips

1. Clothing:

• Footwear is Key: Verona is a walker's paradise. Pack comfortable walking shoes with good traction, as the historic center boasts charming, but often uneven, cobblestone streets. Opt for breathable materials for warmer months and closed-toe shoes for cooler weather.

• Layering is Your Friend: Verona's weather can be unpredictable, especially during spring and fall. Pack layers like lightweight sweaters, long-sleeved shirts, and scarves to adapt to fluctuating temperatures.

• Embrace Versatility: Pack versatile pieces that can be mixed and matched. Think neutral tones like beige, navy, and black, with pops of color in scarves or accessories. This allows you to create multiple outfits without overloading your suitcase.

• Respect the Culture: When visiting churches and religious sites, dress modestly. Pack a lightweight scarf to cover up if needed.

2. Essentials:

• Sun Protection: Verona enjoys plenty of sunshine. Pack a hat with a wide brim and sunglasses with UV protection. Don't forget sunscreen with SPF 30 or higher, and reapply throughout the day, especially during peak sun hours.

• Reusable Water Bottle: Staying hydrated is crucial, especially during the warmer months. Pack a reusable water bottle to avoid single-use plastics and save money. Refill your bottle frequently at fountains or cafes.

• Travel Adapter: Italy uses a two-pronged plug (type F). If you're traveling from a country with a different plug type, pack a universal travel adapter to ensure you can charge your electronic devices.

• Comfortable Crossbody Bag: A secure crossbody bag with a zipper closure is ideal for sightseeing. It keeps your valuables close to your body and helps prevent petty theft.

3. Additional Considerations:

- Swimwear: If your hotel has a pool or you plan on visiting nearby Lake Garda, pack a swimsuit.

- Light Jacket/Raincoat: A lightweight rain jacket or a packable windbreaker can be a lifesaver in case of unexpected showers.

Comfortable Outfit for Travel: Pack a comfortable outfit for your travel day, considering the mode of transportation.

- First-Aid Kit: A small, travel-sized first-aid kit with basic medications like pain relievers, bandages, and antiseptic wipes can come in handy.

- Entertainment: Download some audiobooks, podcasts, or movies to your devices for entertainment during long train journeys or evenings spent relaxing in your hotel room.

4. Remember:

- Check Airline Restrictions: Always check baggage weight and size restrictions for your airline to avoid any last-minute surprises.

- Embrace the Local Style: Verona offers a charming blend of casual and elegant styles. Pack a versatile outfit you can dress up or down depending on the occasion.

For example, a nice pair of dark-wash jeans can be paired with a t-shirt for daytime exploration and dressed up with a blouse and blazer for an evening out.

• Leave Room for Souvenirs: Leave some extra space in your luggage for those irresistible souvenirs you might pick up during your Verona adventure.

Budgeting and Costs

1. Accommodation (per night):

• Budget (hostels, guesthouses): €40-€70

• Mid-Range (hotels with basic amenities): €70-€120

• Luxury (boutique hotels, apartments): €120+

2. Food (per day):

• Budget (picnics, street food): €20-€30

• Mid-Range (casual restaurants, trattorias): €30-€50

• Fine Dining: €50+

3. Transportation:

• Walking (free): Verona is compact and easily explored on foot.

Public Transportation (day pass): €10-€15

- Taxis: Taxis are metered and can be expensive for short trips. Consider them for late-night journeys or carrying heavy luggage.

4. Activities:

- Free Walking Tours: Free with an optional tip at the end.

- Museums and Attractions: Entrance fees typically range from €5 to €20. Consider purchasing a Verona Card for discounted entry to major attractions and free public transportation.

- Opera Tickets: Prices vary depending on the performance, seat location, and season. Expect to pay a premium for peak seasons and popular operas.

5. Additional Expenses:

- Travel Insurance: Prices vary depending on your coverage and trip duration. Budget around €3–€5 per day for basic coverage.

- Souvenirs: Prices can vary widely. Allocate a budget depending on your shopping preferences.

- Entertainment: Factor in costs for evenings out, such as drinks at cafes or attending a concert.

Here's a sample daily budget breakdown (based on mid-range options):

1. Accommodation: €100
2. Food: €40
3. Transportation: €10
4. Activities: €20

Total: €170 per day.

Remember, this is just a starting point. You can adjust it based on your travel style and preferences. Here are some additional tips for budget-conscious travelers:

• Travel During the Off-Season: Accommodation and flight prices tend to be lower during the shoulder seasons (spring and fall) compared to peak summer months.

• Cook Some Meals: Consider staying in an apartment with a kitchen and preparing some meals yourself to save on dining costs.

• Take Advantage of Free Activities: Verona offers plenty of free things to see and do, like exploring the charming piazzas, people-watching in cafes, or attending free cultural events.

• Pack a Reusable Water Bottle: Refill it at fountains or cafes to avoid constantly buying bottled water.

• Walk Whenever Possible: Not only is it free, but walking allows you to truly discover the city's hidden gems and charming backstreets.

Language and Useful Phrases

1. Italian 101:

While English is spoken to some degree in tourist areas, learning a few key Italian phrases goes a long way. It demonstrates respect for the local culture and can enhance your interactions with friendly Veronese people. Here are some must-knows:

• Greetings: Buongiorno (boo-njor-no): Good morning/ or afternoon (until around sunset)

Buonasera (bwona-seh-ra): Good evening Ciao (ciao): Hello/Goodbye (informal)

• Essential Phrases: Grazie (grah-tsee-eh): Thank you Prego (preh-go): You're welcome (also used for "please"). Scusi (scusi): Excuse me Mi scusi (mee scusi): I'm sorry Si (see): Yes No (no): No Per favore (pehr fah-voh-reh): Please Parla inglese? (par-la in-gleh-seh): Do you speak English?

- In Restaurants: Posso avere il conto, per favore? (poh-sso ah-veh-reh eel kon-toh, pehr fah-voh-reh): Can I have the bill, please? Un bicchiere di vino rosso/bianco, per favore (oon bee-kee-eheh dee vee-no rosso/bianco, pehr fah-voh-reh): A glass of red or white wine, please. Mi piacerebbe (mee pee-ah-cheh-reh-beh): I would like...

2. Cultural Nuances:

- Formalities: Italians tend to be more formal than Americans. Using titles like "Signore" (See-nyor-eh) for men and "Signora" (See-nyo-rah) for women is a sign of respect.

- Gestures: Italians are expressive! A simple hand gesture can convey a whole message. However, avoid using overly exaggerated gestures yourself, as it might come across as comical.

- Greetings: A handshake is the standard greeting, with a light kiss on the cheek for close friends or upon introduction.

- Table Manners: Italians take dining seriously. Meals are unhurried affairs, so savor your food and enjoy the company. Tipping is not expected, but a small round up to the nearest Euro is appreciated for exceptional service.

3. Beyond the Basics:

- Learn Basic Numbers: Knowing numbers 1–10 will help you navigate prices, addresses, and bus schedules.

- Embrace the Challenge: Don't be afraid to make mistakes! Italians appreciate your effort to speak their language, and a good laugh can break the ice.

- Learn a Fun Phrase: "Mi piace Verona!" (Mee pee-ah-cheh Verona!) "I love Verona!" is a guaranteed conversation starter.

Connectivity and Internet Access

1. Widespread Wi-Fi:

- Public Squares: The central piazzas, like Piazza delle Erbe and Piazza Bra, often boast free Wi-Fi networks, allowing you to connect while soaking in the vibrant atmosphere.

- Tourist Hubs: Airports, train stations, and popular tourist attractions frequently offer free Wi-Fi for visitor convenience.

- Restaurants and Cafes: Many establishments entice customers with free Wi-Fi. Enjoy a delicious meal and connect with the Internet.

2. Connecting to Public Wi-Fi:

- Network Names: Look for Wi-Fi networks with names like "freewifi@verona" or those indicating the establishment offering the service (e.g., "Caffe Rossi Wi-Fi").

- Login Process: Some networks might require a simple login process, usually involving entering an email address or accepting terms of service.

3. A Word of Caution:

- Avoid Sensitive Transactions: Refrain from online banking, credit card purchases, or accessing sensitive accounts while connected to public Wi-Fi.

- Consider a VPN: A Virtual Private Network encrypts your internet traffic, adding an extra layer of security to public networks.

- Turn Off File Sharing: Disable file sharing on your devices to prevent unauthorized access.

4. Mobile Data:

● Prepaid SIM Cards: Major Italian mobile network operators like TIM, Vodafone, and WindTre offer prepaid SIM cards with data packages. These can be purchased at airports, convenience stores, and mobile phone shops. Prices and data allowances can vary, so compare options before you buy.

● Roaming: If you're traveling from within the European Union (EU), you might be able to use your existing mobile data plan while in Italy, with roaming charges included. However, check with your provider for specific details and potential roaming fees. Data roaming charges can be exorbitant, so a local SIM card is often the more economical option.

5. Choosing the Right Option:

● Light Internet Users: Free Wi-Fi hotspots might suffice for occasional email checks, social media updates, and using navigation apps while connected.

● Heavy Internet Users: Consider purchasing a local SIM card with a data package for uninterrupted connectivity, allowing you to upload photos, stream music, or use GPS navigation freely.

Chapter 3: Getting There

By Air

1. Your Gateway to Verona: Verona Villafranca Airport (VRN)

Verona's main airport, Verona Villafranca Airport (also known as Valerio Catullo Airport), is a convenient and efficient entry point into the city. Located just 5 kilometers (3 miles) from the city center, the airport caters to both domestic and international flights.

2. Major Airlines and Routes:

• European Airlines: Several major European airlines operate flights to Verona, including Alitalia, British Airways, Lufthansa, easyJet, and Volotea. These airlines offer connections from major European cities like London, Paris, Frankfurt, and Amsterdam.

• Low-Cost Carriers: Budget-conscious travelers can rejoice! Low-cost carriers like Ryanair, Wizz Air, and Eurowings offer flights to Verona from various European destinations, making your Verona adventure more affordable.

3. Finding Flights:

● Airline Websites: Check the websites of airlines operating flights to Verona for schedules, fares, and promotions.

● Travel Aggregator Websites: Popular travel aggregator websites like Kayak, Skyscanner, and Google Flights allow you to compare prices and routes from various airlines, often offering deals and discounts.

4. Beyond Verona Airport:

● Venice Marco Polo Airport (VCE): Located approximately 106 kilometers (66 miles) from Verona, Venice Marco Polo Airport offers a wider range of international connections. However, factor in the additional travel time and cost of transportation from Venice to Verona.

● Bologna Guglielmo Marconi Airport (BLQ): This airport is situated about 103 kilometers (64 miles) from Verona and offers another alternative, especially if you find a good deal on flights. Similar to Venice, you'll need to factor in ground transportation costs and travel time.

5. Planning Your Arrival:

- Airport Transportation: Verona Villafranca Airport offers various transportation options to reach the city center:

- Aerobus: A convenient and affordable option, the Aerobus operates regularly between the airport and Verona Porta Nuova train station.

- Taxi: Taxis are readily available at the airport, but be prepared for slightly higher fares compared to public transportation.

- Pre-Booked Private Transfers: For a hassle-free arrival, consider pre-booking a private transfer service that takes you directly to your hotel.

- Luggage Claim: After deplaning, follow the signs for baggage claim to collect your luggage.

- Customs: If you're arriving from a non-EU country, you'll need to pass through customs. Have your passport and any required documents readily available.

6. A Few Extra Tips:

- Book Your Flights in Advance: Especially during peak travel seasons, booking your flights well in advance can help you score better deals.

• Consider Luggage Fees: Some airlines, particularly low-cost carriers, charge extra for checked baggage. Factor this into your budget when comparing flight prices.

By Train

1. Your Arrival Station: Verona Porta Nuova

Verona's main train station, Verona Porta Nuova, is a bustling hub connecting you to various Italian and European destinations. This modern and well-equipped station serves as your gateway to exploring the city's treasures.

2. Connecting to Verona by Train:

• From Major Italian Cities: High-speed trains (operated by both Trenitalia and Italo) connect Verona to major Italian cities like Milan (1 hour 13 minutes), Venice (1 hour 12 minutes), Florence (1 hour 32 minutes), and Rome (under 3 hours). These fast and comfortable trains make Verona an ideal base for exploring northern Italy.

• From European Destinations: Verona is also well-connected to several European cities. EuroCity services offer direct links from Munich and Geneva, while overnight trains provide a comfortable way to arrive from Paris and Vienna.

3. Booking Your Train Tickets:

• Trenitalia Website: The official Trenitalia website (https://www.trenitalia.com/en.html) allows you to search train schedules, fares, and book tickets in advance. The website is available in English.

• Italo Website: Italo, a private train operator, offers an alternative for high-speed train travel within Italy. Check their website (https://www.italotreno.com/it) for schedules, fares, and booking options (also available in English).

• Third-Party Platforms: Websites like https://www.thetrainline.com/ and https://www.rome2rio.com/ can be helpful for comparing train options, schedules, and fares across different operators.

4. Planning Your Arrival:

• Train Station Facilities: Verona Porta Nuova offers a variety of amenities, including luggage lockers, cafes, restaurants, currency exchange offices, and tourist information desks.

- Navigating the Station: The station is well-signposted, making it easy to find your platform and departure gate. Information screens display real-time train arrival and departure times.

- Luggage Claim: Upon arrival, follow signs for "uscita" (exit) and baggage claim to collect your luggage.

- Onward Travel: Verona's city center is a pleasant 20-minute walk from the train station. Alternatively, taxis, buses, and the metro (limited lines) are readily available for onward travel.

5. A Few Extra Tips:

- Purchase Tickets in Advance: Especially during peak travel seasons, booking your train tickets well in advance can help you secure better deals and avoid last-minute stress.

- Consider Train Passes: If you plan on exploring multiple Italian cities by train, consider purchasing a regional or national rail pass, which can offer significant savings compared to buying individual tickets.

By Car

1. Verona's Crossroads: A Network of Motorways

- A4 Serenissima: This east-west motorway, also known as the Venice-Milan motorway, connects Verona to major cities like Venice (east) and Milan (west).

- A22 Modena-Brennero: This north-south motorway links Verona to cities like Modena (south) and Brenner Pass (north) on the border with Austria.

2. Essential Information for Drivers:

- Tolls: Be prepared to pay tolls while driving on motorways in Italy. Most toll roads accept cash and major credit cards. Some rentals might offer prepaid toll boxes for added convenience.

- Speed Limits: Speed limits vary depending on the road type. Generally, the speed limit on motorways is 130 km/h (80 mph), while it's lower on secondary roads and in urban areas.

- ZTL Zones: Many Italian city centers, including Verona's historic core, have restricted traffic zones (ZTL). Unless you have a special permit, avoid driving into these zones. Look for designated parking areas outside the ZTL and explore the city center on foot or by public transportation.

● International Driving Permit (IDP): While not mandatory in Italy, an IDP is highly recommended, especially if you're renting a car.

3. Tips for a Smooth Drive:

● Plan Your Stops: Factor in rest stops, gas stations, and potential traffic delays while planning your journey.

● Be Aware of Road Signs: Pay attention to road signs for directions, speed limits, and ZTL zones.

● Enjoy the Scenery: The drive to Verona offers stunning landscapes, charming towns, and rolling hills. Relax, take breaks to explore, and soak in the Italian countryside.

4. Parking in Verona:

● Public Parking Garages: Several multi-story parking garages are located around the city center. These offer secure parking but can be pricey.

● Park & Ride Lots: Verona has a few Park & Ride facilities on the outskirts of the city, allowing you to leave your car and take public transportation into the city center.

- Street Parking: On-street parking is available in some areas, but be mindful of parking restrictions and designated zones.

Public Transportation Overview

1. The Heartbeat of the City: The Bus Network

- Bus Routes and Schedules: Download the handy "ATV Mobile" app (available for iOS and Android) to access real-time bus arrival information, plan your trip, and purchase tickets online (in Italian only). Alternatively, paper schedules and route maps are available at ATV offices and tourist information centers.

- Tickets and Fares: Tickets can be purchased at newsstands, tobacco shops, vending machines at bus stops, or through the app. Consider purchasing a day ticket (biglietto giornaliero) for unlimited travel within a 24-hour period, ideal for extensive exploration.

2. Beyond the Buses: Exploring Other Options

- Verona Card: This tourist pass combines free entry to major attractions with unlimited travel on ATV buses for a set period (24 or 48 hours). Consider this option if you plan on visiting several attractions and using public transportation frequently.

• Verona Airport Shuttle: A dedicated Aerobus service connects Verona Villafranca Airport (VRN) with Verona Porta Nuova train station, making airport transfers a breeze. Tickets can be purchased on board.

• Taxis: Taxis are readily available throughout the city, especially near train stations and popular tourist areas. They can be convenient for late-night journeys or carrying heavy luggage, but be prepared for higher fares compared to buses.

3. Embrace the Walkability:

Verona's historic city center is remarkably compact and pedestrian-friendly. Lace up your walking shoes and explore charming piazzas, discover hidden alleyways, and stumble upon unexpected gems—all at your own pace. Walking allows you to truly immerse yourself in the city's atmosphere and hidden corners.

4. A Few Extra Tips:

• Learn Basic Italian Phrases: Knowing a few basic Italian phrases like "Quanto costa il biglietto?" (How much is the ticket?) or "Mi scusi, dove si trova la fermata dell'autobus?" (Excuse me, where is the bus stop?) can go a long way.

• Purchase Tickets in Advance: Avoid last-minute scrambling by purchasing tickets for day passes or the Verona Card beforehand.

• Validate Your Ticket: Always validate your ticket upon boarding the bus to avoid fines from inspectors.

• Consider a Bike Rental: For a unique perspective and a bit of exercise, consider renting a bike and exploring the city on two wheels. Several bike rental shops are located in Verona.

Chapter 4: Getting Around Verona

Public Transit: Buses and Taxis

1. The King of the Road: Verona's Bus Network

- Widespread Coverage: The ATV network connects major landmarks, bustling neighborhoods, and even Verona Villafranca Airport (VRN) to the city center.

- Planning Your Journey: Download the user-friendly "ATV Mobile" app (available for iOS and Android) for real-time bus arrival information, route planning, and ticket purchases (the app currently only available in Italian). Alternatively, paper schedules and route maps are available at ATV offices and tourist information centers.

2. Ticketing and Fares:

- Purchasing Tickets: Don't get caught flat-footed! Purchase tickets beforehand at newsstands, tobacco shops, vending machines at bus stops, or through the app (if comfortable using Italian).

- Ticket Validation: Once on board, validate your ticket using the machines near the entrance to avoid fines.

3. Ticketing Options:

- Single Tickets: Ideal for occasional rides, single tickets allow for a single journey within a set time frame (usually 90 minutes).

- Day Tickets (biglietto giornaliero): For a day of extensive exploration, consider a day ticket offering unlimited travel within a 24-hour period.

4. Beyond the Buses: Taxis—Your Knight in Shining Armor (or Car)

- Late-Night Travel: If you're exploring Verona's nightlife and public transportation has ceased operation, taxis are your safe and reliable option for getting back to your hotel.

- Heavy Luggage: Don't struggle with cumbersome suitcases! Taxis are a lifesaver if you're arriving at or departing from Verona Porta Nuova train station with heavy luggage.

- Limited Mobility: For those with limited mobility, taxis provide a comfortable and convenient way to get around the city.

5. Finding Taxis:

• Taxi Ranks: You'll find taxi ranks at major transportation hubs like train stations and airports.

• Hailing a Taxi: While not as common as in other cities, you might be able to hail a taxi on the street, especially near tourist areas. Look for taxis with their roof lights illuminated.

• Pre-Booked Taxis: For guaranteed service, consider pre-booking a taxi through your hotel or a ridesharing app (availability might be limited).

6. A Word on Taxi Fares:

• Metered Fares: Taxis operate on a meter system, so the fare depends on the distance traveled.

• Night Rates: Be aware that night rates apply after a certain time (usually around 10 p.m.), so expect slightly higher fares.

• Tipping: Tipping taxi drivers is not mandatory in Italy, but a small gratuity (rounded up to the nearest Euro) is always appreciated for good service.

7. Choosing Between Buses and Taxis:

For budget-conscious travelers and daytime exploration, the efficient bus network is the clear winner. However, if you find yourself with heavy luggage, require late-night transportation, or have limited mobility, taxis offer a convenient and comfortable alternative.

8. A Few Extra Tips:

• Learn Basic Italian Phrases: A few key phrases like "Mi porta al..." (Take me to...) or "Quanto costa?" (How much does it cost?) can go a long way with taxi drivers.

• Carry Small Change: While taxis might accept credit cards, it's always wise to have small bills on hand for easier fare payment.

• Compare Rates: If hailing a taxi on the street, it doesn't hurt to ask for an estimated fare before getting in.

Bike and Scooter Rentals

1. Pedal Through History: Exploring Verona by Bike

• A Cyclist's Paradise: Verona's historic center is remarkably pedestrian and bicycle-friendly, with dedicated bike lanes and relatively flat terrain. Renting a bike allows you to:

- Explore at Your Own Pace: Unlike guided tours, bikes offer the freedom to stop and linger at your favorite spots, creating a truly personalized itinerary.
- Discover Hidden Gems: Venture beyond the main attractions and discover charming alleyways, tucked-away cafes, and unexpected sights.
- Embrace the Fresh Air: Leave the crowds behind and enjoy a healthy dose of fresh air as you explore the city.

2. Finding the Perfect Bike Rental:

- Types of Bikes: Shops offer various bike options, including city bikes, hybrid bikes, and e-bikes (electric bikes) for those seeking a little extra assistance.
- Rental Duration: Choose a rental duration that suits your needs, from a few hours to multiple days.
- Helmets and Accessories: Ensure the rental shop provides helmets, locks, and any other necessary accessories.
- Location: Consider a shop close to your starting point for convenience.

3. Popular Bike Rental Shops in Verona:

- Itinera Bike & Travel: Located near the Porta Nuova train station, this shop offers various bike options, including e-bikes, with helmets.

- Verona Bike Rental: Situated in the city center, this shop offers city bikes and e-bikes with helmets and locks at affordable rates.

4. Scootering Through Verona: A Touch of Italian Flair

- Cover More Ground: Compared to bikes, scooters allow you to explore farther distances and reach destinations outside the city center more efficiently.

- Experience the Open Road: Venture out to charming towns and scenic landscapes surrounding Verona on a scooter adventure.

Important Considerations Before Renting a Scooter:

- International Driver's Permit (IDP): While not mandatory in Italy, an IDP is highly recommended, especially if you're renting a scooter with an engine displacement exceeding 50 cc.

- Scooter License Requirements: Scooter rental requirements can vary. Ensure you possess the necessary license category to operate the scooter you wish to rent.

• Traffic Regulations: Familiarize yourself with Verona's traffic regulations, including speed limits, parking zones, and ZTL zones (limited traffic zones) where scooters might be restricted.

5. Scooter Rental Options in Verona:

• Scooter Selection: Look for a company offering various scooter sizes and engine displacements to suit your experience level.

• Insurance Options: Inquire about insurance coverage and consider purchasing additional insurance for peace of mind.

• Safety Gear: Ensure the rental company provides helmets and any other necessary safety gear.

6. A Few Extra Tips:

• Plan Your Route: Map out your intended route beforehand, considering designated scooter parking areas and avoiding ZTL zones.

• Ride Defensively: Be aware of your surroundings, ride defensively, and respect traffic regulations for a safe and enjoyable experience.

Walking: Exploring the City on Foot

1. A Journey Through Time: Exploring Verona's Walkable Heart

• Unveiling Hidden Gems: Beyond the main attractions, Verona boasts charming side streets, tucked-away courtyards, and unexpected architectural delights. Walking allows you to wander freely and stumble upon hidden gems that might be missed by a bus or car.

• Soak Up the Atmosphere: The best way to truly immerse yourself in Verona's vibrant atmosphere is to walk its streets. Listen to the murmur of conversations at cafes, smell the aroma of freshly baked bread from local bakeries, and feel the energy of the city around you.

• Discover Architectural Details: Verona's architectural beauty unfolds as you walk. Take your time to admire ornate doorways, hidden frescoes, and architectural details that might be missed while rushing by on public transportation.

2. Planning Your Walking Tour:

• Comfortable Shoes: Verona's streets are mostly cobbled, so prioritize comfortable walking shoes with good grip.

• Pick a Theme: Are you interested in Shakespeare's Romeo and Juliet? Or perhaps Roman history? Thematic walking tours allow you to delve deeper into specific aspects of Verona's rich past.

• Consider a Guided Walking Tour: For a more in-depth experience, join a guided walking tour led by a knowledgeable local guide. These tours offer historical insights and anecdotes you might miss on your own.

3. A Few Suggested Walking Routes:

• From the Arena to Castelvecchio: This route takes you past the iconic Verona Arena, the bustling Piazza delle Erbe, and the impressive Castelvecchio bridge, offering a glimpse into Verona's Roman and medieval history.

• In the Footsteps of Romeo and Juliet: Follow in the footsteps of Shakespeare's star-crossed lovers, visiting Juliet's balcony, Casa di Giulietta (Juliet's House), and charming piazzas mentioned in the play.

• A Walk Along the Adige River: Enjoy a scenic stroll along the banks of the River Adige, offering stunning views of the city and the Ponte Pietra, the oldest bridge in Verona.

4. Walking Beyond the City Walls:

● Giardino Giusti: Venture outside the city walls and explore this beautiful 16th-century garden, offering tranquil green spaces, panoramic views, and hidden grottos.

● Castel San Pietro: Hike up to Castel San Pietro for breathtaking panoramic views of the city and the surrounding countryside. The climb is manageable, and the reward is worth the effort.

5. A Few Extra Tips:

● Carry a Water Bottle: Stay hydrated, especially during warmer months. Refill your water bottle at public fountains found throughout the city.

● Pack Light: Opt for a comfortable backpack to carry essentials like sunscreen, a hat, and a camera.

● Take Breaks: Verona is a city meant to be savored. Take breaks at cafes, people-watch in piazzas, and enjoy the relaxed Italian pace of life.

Chapter 5: Accommodation Options

Luxury Abodes

1. JK Rooms Verona (5-star): Nestled in a meticulously restored 15th-century building, this boutique hotel embodies understated elegance. Step into a world where history whispers on the walls and modern luxury pampers your every need. Each room is meticulously designed, offering a unique blend of exposed brickwork, original frescoes, and plush furnishings. Unwind in the tranquil spa featuring a hammam and sauna, or indulge in a gourmet culinary experience at the on-site restaurant, Incanto. The hotel's central location places you steps away from major attractions and vibrant piazzas, allowing you to explore Verona's rich tapestry at your own pace. Price: Starting at €520 per night.

2. Palazzo Victoria (5-star): Nestled in the heart of Verona's historic center, this 16th-century palace boasts a captivating blend of Renaissance charm and modern

luxury. Unwind in opulent rooms featuring frescoed ceilings, marble bathrooms, and plush furnishings. Savor exquisite meals at the renowned La Vecchia Verona restaurant or sip cocktails on the rooftop terrace with breathtaking city views. Expect exceptional service and a truly unforgettable stay. Price: Starting at €450 per night.

3. JK Rooms Verona (5-star): This boutique hotel housed in a restored 15th-century building embodies understated elegance. Each room is meticulously designed, offering a unique blend of modern amenities and historical charm. Relax in the tranquil spa featuring a hammam and sauna, or indulge in a gourmet culinary experience at the on-site restaurant, Incanto. The hotel's central location places you steps away from major attractions and vibrant piazzas. Price: Starting at €520 per night.

4. Hotel Scalzi (5-star): Experience unparalleled luxury at this historic hotel, meticulously restored and boasting a rich heritage dating back to the 19th century. Lavish rooms offer a haven of comfort with high ceilings, plush furniture, and marble bathrooms. Savor delectable Italian cuisine at the renowned Il Giardino Restaurant or unwind in the elegant bar. The hotel boasts an on-site spa

and a rooftop terrace with panoramic city views. Price: Starting at €480 per night.

5. Villa Arcole (5-star): Nestled outside the city center, this 18th-century villa offers a luxurious escape. Tranquil gardens, a sparkling pool, and an on-site Michelin-starred restaurant create an oasis of relaxation. Spacious rooms boast elegant décor and modern amenities. Indulge in the spa or explore the surrounding vineyards. Price: Starting at €620 per night (often including breakfast).

Mid-Range Gems

1. Locanda al Vescovo (4-star): This charming hotel housed in a 16th-century building offers a delightful blend of history and modern comfort. Located in a peaceful corner near the Adige River, it provides a respite from the city's hustle and bustle. Spacious and elegantly decorated rooms offer a tranquil space to relax. Enjoy delicious breakfasts prepared with local ingredients and friendly service from the attentive staff. Price: Starting at €180 per night.

2. Antico Teatro 11 Suites & Spa (4-star): Situated in a historic building close to the Roman Theatre, this hotel exudes a sophisticated and elegant atmosphere. Modern, well-appointed suites offer a comfortable haven. Pamper yourself at the on-site spa, which features a sauna, Turkish bath, and a range of massage treatments. Enjoy a rooftop terrace with panoramic views and a charming courtyard for al fresco dining. Price: Starting at €210 per night.

3. Boutique Hotel Aurora (3-star): This charming hotel offers a warm and inviting atmosphere in a central location near Piazza Bra. Modern, tastefully decorated rooms provide a comfortable space to relax. Enjoy delicious breakfasts prepared with fresh, local ingredients and friendly service from the attentive staff. The hotel boasts a rooftop terrace with stunning city views, perfect for soaking up the atmosphere. Price: Starting at €150 per night.

4. Le Suite di Giulietta (4-star): Situated near Juliet's House, this charming hotel offers a romantic and elegant atmosphere. Each suite is uniquely decorated, featuring exposed brick walls, modern furnishings, and some even

boasting balconies overlooking the iconic courtyard. Relax in the rooftop Jacuzzi or indulge in a delicious breakfast on the terrace. Price: Starting at €230 per night.

5. Corte Realdi (4-star): This historic hotel, dating back to the 14th century, exudes Venetian charm in the heart of Verona. Rooms that are roomy and attractive offer a cozy retreat. Enjoy a rooftop bar with panoramic city views and a renowned restaurant serving traditional Veronese cuisine. The on-site spa offers a haven for relaxation. Price: Starting at €190 per night.

Budget-Friendly Stays

1. Ostello Verona (Hostel): This vibrant hostel offers a social and budget-friendly stay experience. Choose from dorm rooms or private rooms, all featuring comfortable beds and clean facilities. Mingle with fellow travelers in the common areas, enjoy a delicious breakfast, and take advantage of the hostel's tours and activities. The central location puts you close to all major attractions. Price: Starting at €30 per night for a dorm bed.

2. Ai Santi B&B (B&B): This cozy B&B offers a warm and welcoming atmosphere close to the Castelvecchio bridge. Simple but clean and comfortable rooms provide a good night's sleep. Enjoy freshly baked pastries and local specialties for breakfast, served in a charming dining room. The friendly owner can offer recommendations and tips for exploring the city. Price: Starting at €60 per night for a double room.

3. Shakespeare Rooms Verona (Guest House): Situated a short walk from Juliet's House, this family-run guest house offers a comfortable and affordable stay. Choose from simple rooms with shared bathrooms or en-suite options. Enjoy a basic breakfast and friendly service from the owners. The location is perfect for exploring Verona's romantic side. Price: Starting at €55 per night for a double room.

4. Locanda Scaligero (Guest House): This family-run guest house offers a warm and welcoming atmosphere near the Arena. Simple yet comfortable rooms provide a good night's sleep. Enjoy a delicious breakfast featuring local specialties served in a charming courtyard. The friendly staff can offer recommendations for exploring

the city. Price: Starting at €70 per night for a double room.

5. Residenza Al Sirmione (B&B): Situated a short walk from the Castelvecchio Bridge, this B&B offers a modern and stylish haven. The accommodations are cozy and well-kept, with all the necessities. Enjoy a continental breakfast served in a bright breakfast room. The central location makes exploring Verona's heart a breeze. Price: Starting at €50 per night for a double room.

Chapter 6: Top Attractions

Must-See Sights

1. Stepping Back in Time: Verona's Roman Legacy

- Arena di Verona: This awe-inspiring Roman amphitheater, dating back to the 1st century AD, is the crown jewel of Verona. Imagine gladiatorial battles of old, or feel the thrill of attending a world-renowned opera performance under the starlit sky. Explore the backstage areas and hidden passageways through guided tours, or simply marvel at its architectural grandeur.

- Porta Borsari: This imposing Roman city gate, erected in the 1st century AD, served as the main entrance to the ancient city. Admire the intricate details of the arches and sculptures, remnants of Verona's glorious Roman past. Take a moment to imagine the bustling trade routes and historical figures who once passed through these grand gates.

- Ponte Pietra: Verona's oldest bridge, dating back to Roman times, spans the Adige River. Stroll across its ancient stones and soak in the picturesque views of the river and the city skyline. This bridge whispers tales of bygone eras and offers a peaceful escape from the city's energy.

2. A Walk Through Medieval Charm: Exploring Verona's Piazzas and Palaces

• Piazza delle Erbe: This lively square, once the Roman forum, is now a bustling marketplace. Wander through stalls overflowing with fresh produce, local crafts, and regional specialties. Admire the imposing Torre della Erbe (Clock Tower) and the nearby Casa Mazzanti, a captivating example of medieval architecture.

• Piazza dei Signori: This elegant square, also known as Piazza Dante, is the political heart of Verona. Stand in awe of the Palazzo del Comune (Town Hall), adorned with intricate carvings and a majestic lion statue. Pay homage to the statue of Dante Alighieri, the famous poet, and soak in the atmosphere of this historic square.

• Castelvecchio: This imposing medieval fortress, originally built as a scaliger family residence, now houses the Castelvecchio Museum. Explore its ramparts and courtyards, or delve into the museum's rich collection of art, including paintings, sculptures, and weapons, offering a glimpse into Verona's artistic heritage.

3. A Touch of Romance: Following in the Footsteps of Romeo and Juliet

- Casa di Giulietta (Juliet's House): A must-see for any hopeless romantic, this 14th-century house is believed to have belonged to the Capulet family, Juliet's kin in Shakespeare's play. Touch the iconic balcony, scrawl a message on the wall, or simply stand beneath it and imagine the star-crossed lovers' fateful encounter.

- Tomba di Giulietta (Juliet's Tomb): Descend into the crypt beneath the former San Francesco al Corso church to see Juliet's sarcophagus, a replica of the one depicted in the play. While the historical accuracy remains debated, the tomb offers a poignant reminder of the enduring power of love.

- Cortile dei Capuleti (Courtyard of the Capulets): While not Juliet's actual house, this residence belonged to the Capello family, a rival clan to the Montagues in Shakespeare's play. Admire the elegant architecture, and imagine the family feuds that unfolded within these walls.

4. Beyond the Classics: Unveiling Verona's Hidden Gems

• Giardino Giusti: Escape the city bustle and find tranquility at this 16th-century Renaissance garden. Wander through manicured hedges, explore hidden grottos adorned with statues, and admire the breathtaking panoramic views of the city from the top of the hill.

• Duomo (Verona Cathedral): This majestic cathedral, with its Romanesque facade and Gothic interior, boasts a rich history dating back to the 12th century. Admire the artwork, explore the baptistery, and experience the serenity of this sacred space.

• Teatro Romano: Verona's Roman theater, nestled against a hillside, predates the Arena. While partially ruined, it offers a glimpse into the city's ancient entertainment culture. Enjoy stunning views of the city from the theater's upper tiers, and imagine the performances that once took place here.

Arena di Verona

1. A Journey Through Time: From Roman Grandeur to Modern Marvel

• A Legacy Etched in Stone: Built in the 1st century AD, the Arena di Verona is the third-largest Roman amphitheater still standing. Imagine the bustling crowds of the Roman era, drawn to witness gladiatorial contests, public executions, and theatrical performances. Marvel at the elliptical structure, built from pink and white limestone, and appreciate the engineering marvel that has withstood centuries.

• Deciphering the Architectural Grandeur: Explore the intricate details of the Arena's architecture. The caves (seating area) once accommodated up to 30,000 spectators, offering tiered sections based on social status. The orchestra pit, originally the stage for performances, now houses the modern stage machinery. Gaze upwards at the intricate network of arches, the vomitoria (exits), and the velarium, a retractable awning that once protected the audience from the elements.

- A Stage Reborn: From Gladiatorial Games to Operatic Glories: The Arena's history is a fascinating tapestry. While gladiatorial contests ceased in the 5th century, the venue continued to host a variety of events, including jousting tournaments and religious ceremonies. However, it was the 19th century that ushered in a golden age. In 1913, the first opera performance, a spectacular production of Verdi's Aida, breathed new life into the Arena. Since then, it has become a legendary open-air opera venue, attracting renowned singers, conductors, and opera companies from around the world.

2. Experiencing the Arena di Verona: A Multi-Sensory Journey

- Witnessing Operatic Magic: The Arena's true magic unfolds during the summer opera festival, held from June to September. Imagine the electrifying atmosphere as thousands gather under the starlit sky, captivated by a world-renowned opera. The sheer scale of the production, with its elaborate sets, powerful voices, and a live orchestra, creates an unforgettable experience.

- A Guided Exploration: Delve deeper into the Arena's history with a guided tour. Explore backstage areas, hidden passageways, and the camerini (dressing rooms) where legendary performers have prepared for their grand entrances. Learn about the intricate stage machinery and the challenges of open-air production. These tours offer a unique glimpse into the world behind the scenes.

• A Self-Guided Adventure: Even without an opera performance, the Arena is an awe-inspiring sight. Wander through the caves, imagining the roar of the crowds, or climb to the top tiers for breathtaking panoramic views of Verona. Purchase a combined ticket to access the Arena and the adjoining Museo Archeologico (Archaeological Museum) to learn more about Verona's Roman legacy.

Juliet's House (Casa di Giulietta)

1. A Journey Through Time: Fact and Fiction Intertwine

• The House and the Capulets: The 14th-century building belonged to the Capello family, possibly distant relatives of the Capulets from Shakespeare's play. While the historical Juliet may not have resided here, the association with the play has cemented the house's place in Verona's romantic narrative.

- A Courtyard Steeped in Legend: Step into the famed courtyard, the setting for Romeo's serenade in the play. Admire the well and the bronze statue of Juliet, a popular spot for touching her right breast for good luck in love. While the tradition is relatively recent, it adds to the romantic atmosphere.

- Climbing to the Balcony: Ascend the stone staircase to the balcony, the iconic scene of Romeo professing his love. While the balcony's architectural style doesn't quite match the Elizabethan period, it has become a symbol of yearning and forbidden love. Snap a photo, recreate the scene from the play, or simply soak in the atmosphere.

2. Beyond the Romance: Unveiling the House's Secrets

- A Glimpse into Medieval Life: Explore the house beyond the courtyard and balcony. The interior rooms feature period furniture, frescoes, and a collection of Shakespearian memorabilia. Imagine the lives of the Capello family and how they might have used these spaces.

- The Wall of Love: Located in a side alley, this wall is plastered with love notes and messages left by visitors from around the world. Write your own message, expressing your hopes and dreams for love, and add your voice to the global tapestry of romance.

- Juliet's Secretaries: A unique tradition allows visitors to write letters to Juliet, pouring their hearts out about love and relationships. A team of volunteers, known as "Juliet's Secretaries," responds to these letters, offering words of comfort and advice.

3. A Memorable Experience: Fact or Fiction, Love Endures

Casa di Giulietta may not be the historical residence of Shakespeare's Juliet, but it has become a powerful symbol of love and longing. Whether you're a die-hard romantic, a history buff, or simply curious, the house offers a unique experience. Touch the balcony, whisper a message on the wall, or simply stand in the courtyard, letting the magic of Verona weave its spell.

Piazza delle Erbe

1. A Walk Through History: From Roman Forum to Bustling Marketplace

• A Legacy Etched in Stone: Piazza delle Erbe's history stretches back to Roman times, when it served as the city's forum, a central gathering place. Even today, remnants of the past remain. The imposing Torre della Erbe (Clock Tower), dating back to the 14th century, dominates the square, its astronomical clock is a marvel of medieval engineering. Admire the nearby Casa Mazzanti, a captivating example of medieval architecture with its crenellated facade and ornate windows.

• A Feast for the Senses: The true magic of Piazza delle Erbe unfolds in its present-day incarnation as a bustling marketplace. Stalls overflow with an abundance of fresh, seasonal produce. Towering pyramids of colorful vegetables, glistening fruits, and fragrant herbs create a feast for the eyes. Local artisans showcase their wares, from hand-woven linens and intricate leather goods to traditional jewelry and hand-painted ceramics. The aroma of freshly baked bread, cured meats, and local cheeses mingles with the scent of flowers, creating a truly sensory experience.

- A Social Hub: Where Life Unfolds: Piazza delle Erbe is more than just a market – it's a social hub. Locals gather for their daily shopping, catching up with friends and neighbors. Street performers entertain the crowds with music, juggling, and acrobatics. Cafes lining the square offer a chance to rest your weary legs, people-watch, and soak in the atmosphere over a cup of espresso or a glass of local wine. The energy is infectious, a celebration of life and community.

2. Beyond the Market Stalls: Unveiling Hidden Gems

- Fontana del Nettuno (Fountain of Neptune): This 16th-century fountain, adorned with a statue of the sea god Neptune, adds a touch of grandeur to the square. Legend has it that tossing a coin into the fountain ensures your return to Verona.

- Palazzo Maffei: A captivating example of Renaissance architecture, this palace features a beautiful facade adorned with statues and bas-reliefs. Explore its elegant courtyard or admire it from a cafe table, adding a touch of history to your market experience.

• Lamberti Tower: Standing tall next to the Piazza delle Erbe, the Lamberti Tower offers panoramic views of Verona. Climb the winding staircase to the top and be rewarded with breathtaking vistas of the city's rooftops, piazzas, and the Arena in the distance.

Castelvecchio and Ponte Scaligero

1. Castelvecchio: A Fortress Steeped in History

• A Scaliger Legacy: Built in the 14th century by the Della Scala (Scaliger) family, the ruling dynasty of Verona, Castelvecchio served as a military stronghold and a residence. Explore the imposing towers, adorned with the Scaliger coat of arms, and imagine the soldiers who once patrolled the ramparts.

• A Journey Through Time: Step inside the castle walls and delve into its fascinating history. The Castelvecchio Museum houses an impressive collection of art, from paintings by Veronese masters like Tintoretto and Veronese to sculptures, weapons, and archaeological artifacts. Each piece tells a story, offering a glimpse into Verona's artistic heritage and military prowess.

• A Walk Through Fortifications: Explore the castle's courtyards, climb the defensive walkways, and admire the crenellated walls. Descend into the underground passages and imagine the soldiers who once used them for surprise attacks. The castle's architecture is a testament to medieval military engineering, offering a captivating glimpse into the art of defense.

2. Ponte Scaligero: A Bridge Fortified

• A Gateway to Power: Leading across the Adige River, Ponte Scaligero, also known as Castelvecchio Bridge, served as a vital defensive structure. The bridge, with its distinctive crenellated towers and fortified arches, formed a crucial part of the city's defenses, controlling access to the castle.

• A Walk Through History: Stroll across the bridge's cobbled walkway, imagining the clatter of horses' hooves and the weight of armored soldiers marching across. Admire the views of the river and the city skyline from the bridge's vantage point. Notice the intricate details of the stonework, a testament to the skill of medieval craftsmen.

- A Symbol of Resilience: Ponte Scaligero has witnessed centuries of history. It has withstood floods, battles, and the test of time. Its resilience stands as a symbol of Verona's strength and determination.

3. A Combined Experience: Unveiling the Power of Defense

Castelvecchio and Ponte Scaligero are best experienced together. Imagine the soldiers stationed on the bridge, guarding the approach to the castle. Walk through the castle's halls, picturing the battles that may have unfolded within its walls. Together, these structures paint a vivid picture of Verona's turbulent past and its unwavering spirit.

4. Beyond the Fortifications:

- Castelvecchio Bridge at Night: In the evenings, the bridge is illuminated, casting a magical glow over the river and the city. Take a stroll along the riverbank and admire the bridge's beauty bathed in golden light.

- Castelvecchio Museum Tours: The museum offers guided tours that delve deeper into the history of the castle and its collection. Learn about the Scaliger family, the art on display, and the role the castle played in Verona's past.

Chapter 7: Historical and Cultural Highlights

Verona Cathedral (Duomo di Verona)

1. A Walk Through Time: From Humble Beginnings to Majestic Cathedral

- A Legacy of Faith: The Duomo's history stretches back to the 4th century, with the first church standing on the site. However, the present structure was built in the 12th century on the foundations of earlier Christian basilicas. Witness the evolution of architectural styles, from the Romanesque facade to the Gothic influences within.

- A Facade that Tells a Story: The Duomo's exterior, constructed from red Verona marble, is a masterpiece of Romanesque architecture. Admire the intricate details of the sculptures, depicting biblical scenes and religious figures. The central rose window, with its geometric patterns, adds a touch of elegance. Notice the stark contrast between the unfinished facade and the completed bell tower, offering a glimpse into the cathedral's long history.

- Stepping into a Sanctuary: Cross the threshold and enter a world of serenity. The soaring ceilings, supported by massive columns, create an awe-inspiring atmosphere. Light filters through stained-glass windows, casting colorful hues onto the stone floor. The simple yet elegant design fosters a sense of peace and tranquility, inviting contemplation and prayer.

2. A Treasure Trove of Art: Unveiling Artistic Gems

- Masterful Paintings: The Duomo houses an impressive collection of art. Seek out Titian's masterpiece, "Assumption of the Virgin," a magnificent depiction of the Virgin Mary's ascent to heaven. Other notable works include paintings by Tintoretto and Veronese, showcasing the artistic legacy of the region.

- Sculptural Delights: Look for the captivating baptismal font by Master Brioloto, a masterpiece of Romanesque sculpture depicting scenes from the life of Jesus. Admire the intricate stone carvings and statues adorning the chapels and altars, each piece adding to the artistic richness of the cathedral.

• A Chapter Library Steeped in History: Don't miss the Biblioteca Capitolare, the Chapter Library, considered one of the oldest libraries in existence. Its collection boasts ancient manuscripts, early printed books, and priceless religious artifacts, offering a glimpse into Verona's intellectual and spiritual heritage.

3. A Place for Peace and Reflection:

The Duomo is more than just a museum of art and architecture – it's a place of active worship. Witness a mass, light a candle in prayer, or simply sit in quiet contemplation. The serene atmosphere provides a refuge from the city's bustle, offering a space for spiritual renewal and reflection.

4. Beyond the Cathedral Walls:

• The Cloister: Attached to the Duomo is a hidden gem—the 12th-century cloister. This peaceful haven features a series of small columns and arches, offering a tranquil escape from the cathedral's grandeur. Explore the courtyard and admire the mosaics from earlier churches that adorn the floor.

• Nearby Churches: Verona boasts a wealth of churches, each with its own unique character. Consider visiting the nearby Basilica di Sant'Anastasia, known for its impressive frescoes and sculptures, or the Chiesa di San Giorgio in Braida, a beautiful example of Renaissance architecture.

Basilica of San Zeno

1. A Journey Through Time: From Humble Beginnings to Romanesque Glory

• A Saint's Legacy: The Basilica di San Zeno stands on the site of an earlier church built in the 4th century to honor Verona's patron saint, Saint Zeno. The present structure, however, was constructed between the 10th and 12th centuries, showcasing the peak of Romanesque architecture in Northern Italy.

• A Lombard Legacy: The basilica's architectural style reflects the influence of the Lombard people, who ruled much of northern Italy during the Middle Ages. Admire the use of red brick and creamy-colored tuff stone, which create a distinctive visual texture. The emphasis on geometric shapes, round arches, and sculpted details epitomizes the Romanesque style.

• A Facade that Tells a Story: Step in front of the basilica and marvel at its imposing facade. The central doorway, adorned with intricate bronze panels depicting scenes from the life of Christ, is a masterpiece of Romanesque metalwork. The rose window above, with its geometric patterns, symbolizes the wheel of fortune and the cyclical nature of life. Gazing upwards, admire the slender bell tower, adding a touch of verticality to the facade's horizontal emphasis.

2. Stepping into a Sacred Space: Unveiling Artistic Delights

• A Soaring Interior: Cross the threshold and be enveloped by the basilica's awe-inspiring atmosphere. The high vaulted ceiling, supported by massive columns, creates a sense of spaciousness.

The simple yet elegant design fosters a sense of reverence and invites prayerful reflection.

• A Pala Fit for a Saint: One of the basilica's artistic highlights is the Pala di San Zeno by Andrea Mantegna, a masterpiece of Renaissance painting. This large altarpiece depicts scenes from the life of Saint Zeno and is considered one of the most important religious paintings in Northern Italy.

• Crypt and Cloister Secrets: Descend into the crypt, a fascinating space with Romanesque columns and sarcophagi. Explore the cloister, a tranquil haven featuring a peaceful garden and a small Romanesque chapel. Look for remnants of frescoes and architectural details that whisper tales of the basilica's long history.

3. Beyond the Artistic Treasures: A Spiritual Sanctuary

• A Place of Active Worship: The Basilica di San Zeno remains an active church. Witness a mass, light a candle in prayer, or simply sit in quiet contemplation. The serene atmosphere provides a refuge from the city's bustle, offering a space for spiritual renewal and connection with the local community.

• The Legend of Romeo and Juliet: While historical accuracy is debated, a tradition suggests the crypt may have been the location of Romeo and Juliet's secret wedding in Shakespeare's play. Whether fact or fiction, the association adds a touch of romantic intrigue to the basilica's history.

Roman Theatre and Archaeological Museum

1. The Roman Theatre: A Stage Set in Stone

• A Legacy Unearthed: While the exact date of construction remains debated, the Roman Theatre is estimated to have been built in the 1st century BC. Buried for centuries under layers of earth and buildings, it was only partially unearthed in the 19th century. Imagine the excitement of archaeologists as they brought this ancient marvel back to light.

• A Glimpse into Roman Entertainment: Explore the theater's layout, imagining the tiered seating areas (cavea) that once accommodated up to 30,000 spectators. The orchestra pit, originally a stage for performances, now provides an awe-inspiring vantage point. Imagine the stage (scaenae frons), adorned with elaborate backdrop scenery, and hear the roar of the crowd as gladiatorial contests or theatrical productions unfolded.

- A Walk Through Time: Ascend the cavea, imagining the social hierarchy reflected in the seating arrangements. Wealthier citizens enjoyed cushioned seats closer to the stage, while the less privileged sat higher up. Notice the intricate details of the vomitoria (exits) that allowed for efficient crowd control.

2. The Archaeological Museum: Treasures Unearthed

- A Testament to Daily Life: Housed in the former Gesuati monastery built upon the theater's ruins, the Archaeological Museum offers a glimpse into daily life in Roman Verona. Explore a fascinating collection of artifacts, including sculptures, mosaics, bronzes, and ceramics. Each piece tells a story, from the intricate details of religious statues to the everyday objects used by ordinary citizens.

- A Journey Through Time: The museum's collection is chronologically arranged, taking you on a journey through Verona's Roman past. Admire impressive funerary statues depicting wealthy citizens in their finest attire. Marvel at the intricate mosaics that once adorned the floors of Roman villas. Study the weaponry used by

Roman soldiers and imagine the battles they may have fought.

• A Bridge Between Eras: The museum cleverly integrates the ruins of the theater into its exhibits. Walkways meander through the archaeological site, offering a unique perspective of the theater's structure and allowing you to connect the artifacts with their original context.

3. Beyond the Ruins and Relics: A Multi-Sensory Experience

• Reimagined Performances: During the summer months, the Roman Theatre comes alive with open-air performances. Imagine the magic of witnessing an opera or a play under the starlit sky, the ancient stage breathing new life with contemporary artistry.

• Panoramic City Views: Climb to the top tiers of the cavea and be rewarded with breathtaking 360-degree views of Verona. From the red-tiled rooftops to the majestic Arena in the distance, the panorama offers a captivating perspective of the city.

• Interactive Exhibits: The museum incorporates interactive displays that bring history to life. Imagine yourself as a Roman citizen dressed up in replica clothing or testing your skills at a virtual gladiatorial combat game. These interactive elements cater to visitors of all ages and learning styles.

The Scaliger Tombs

1. A Dynasty Etched in Stone: A Legacy of Power

- The Della Scala Domination: From the 13th to the 14th centuries, the Scaligeri family ruled Verona with an iron fist. These tombs, built between the late 13th and late 14th centuries, were a way for the family to showcase their power and prestige even in death.

- Five Tombs, Five Personalities: Explore the five main arcaded tombs, each dedicated to a prominent member of the Della Scala dynasty. The most famous is the elaborate tomb of Cangrande I della Scala, a valiant leader who brought peace and prosperity to Verona. Other tombs, like that of Alberto I, showcase intricate carvings depicting religious and heraldic symbols.

- Gothic Grandeur: The Scaliger Tombs are prime examples of Gothic architecture in Verona. Admire the soaring canopies (baldachins) supported by slender columns. Look for the intricate details of the sculptures, featuring heraldic griffins, lions, and hunting scenes. The use of pink and white marble adds a touch of elegance to the overall structure.

2. A Journey Through Symbolism: Decoding the Tombs

- Equestrian Statues: A Symbol of Power: Crowning each tomb is a magnificent equestrian statue of the deceased ruler, depicting them in full armor, astride their warhorse. This powerful image symbolizes the deceased's military prowess and leadership qualities.

- Sarcophagi and Reliefs: Stories Carved in Stone Below the equestrian statues lie elaborately decorated sarcophagi. These are adorned with bas-reliefs that tell stories about the deceased's life and accomplishments. Look for depictions of battles won, cities conquered, and acts of piety.

- Canine Companions: A Mark of Loyalty A unique feature of the Scaliger Tombs is the presence of statues of dogs guarding the sarcophagi. These loyal companions symbolize fidelity, a quality highly valued by the Scaligeri family.

3. Beyond the Grandiose Facade: A Look Inside

- A Glimpse into the Past: While the tombs were originally open, for preservation purposes, they are now enclosed by wrought iron fences. However, on occasion, the courtyards housing the tombs are opened to the public, offering a rare glimpse inside. Imagine the opulent decorations and funerary objects that may have adorned the interior spaces.

- The Courtyard Setting: The Scaliger Tombs are situated within two courtyards. While the larger one houses the more elaborate tombs, the smaller one features the simpler sarcophagi of other Scaligeri family members. The courtyards themselves add to the atmosphere, creating a sense of solemnity and grandeur.

4. A Legacy That Endures: The Significance of the Scaliger Tombs

- A Bridge Between Eras: The Scaliger Tombs stand as a powerful link between Verona's medieval past and its present. They offer a window into the artistic styles, political power dynamics, and religious beliefs of the time.

- Artistic Masterpieces: Beyond their historical significance, the tombs are masterpieces of Gothic art. The intricate details, the skillful use of materials, and the sheer scale of the monuments leave a lasting impression on visitors.

- A Must-See for History Buffs and Art Lovers: The Scaliger Tombs are a mandatory stop for anyone interested in Verona's history or Gothic architecture. They offer a unique perspective on the city's past and a chance to marvel at the artistic achievements of the Scaligeri era.

Chapter 8: Exploring Verona Neighborhoods and Districts

Centro Storico (Historic Center)

1. A Walk Through Time: Layers of History Unveiled

• Roman Foundations: Verona's Roman roots are evident in the layout of the Centro Storico. The main pedestrian artery, Corso Porta Borsari, follows the path of the ancient Roman decumanus, a major east-west road. Traces of Roman structures, like the Porta Borsari city gate, stand as testaments to the city's early beginnings.

• Medieval Magic: As you delve deeper into the Centro Storico, the influence of the Middle Ages becomes apparent. Towering stone houses adorned with coats of arms and narrow alleyways create a labyrinthine charm. Piazza delle Erbe, once a Roman forum, now brims with a bustling market, a sensory experience reminiscent of medieval marketplaces.

- Renaissance Refinement: The influence of the Renaissance is evident in the elegant palazzos lining the main streets. Admire the ornate facades of the Palazzo Maffei, with its intricate sculptures and balconies, or the Palazzo della Gran Guardia, a masterpiece of 16th-century architecture.

2. A Feast for the Senses: Indulge in Local Delights

- Culinary Delights Around Every Corner: The Centro Storico is a paradise for foodies. From hidden trattorias serving traditional Veronese cuisine to lively cafes offering fresh pasta and local wines, there's something for every palate. Indulge in a plate of "bigoli" (thick spaghetti) with ragù sauce, savor a slice of pandoro (Verona's Christmas cake), or sip on a glass of Valpolicella, a renowned local wine.

- Aromatherapy on the Streets: As you stroll through the Centro Storico, enticing aromas waft from bakeries, pizzerias, and specialty shops. The scent of freshly baked bread mingles with the sweetness of pastries and the rich aroma of cured meats, creating a symphony of delicious smells.

- A Visual Feast in Every Piazza: Each piazza in the Centro Storico offers a visual feast. Piazza delle Erbe overflows with colorful displays of fresh produce and local crafts. Piazza Bra, the city's largest square, provides a stage for street performers and musicians, adding a touch of vibrancy to the atmosphere. The iconic Arena, a Roman amphitheater, dominates the skyline, offering a constant reminder of Verona's ancient heritage.

3. Beyond the Tourist Trail: Unveiling Hidden Gems

- Cortile del Mercato Vecchio: Tucked away in a corner of the Centro Storico lies the Cortile del Mercato Vecchio, a hidden courtyard with a fascinating history. This former market square now provides a tranquil oasis, with cafes and shops lining its arcades.

- Giardino Giusti: Escape the hustle and bustle of the city streets and seek refuge in the Giardino Giusti, a delightful Renaissance garden. Explore its manicured lawns, hidden grottoes, and stunning views of the city from its elevated terraces.

- Juliet's Balcony: No visit to Verona's Centro Storico is complete without a pilgrimage to Casa di Giulietta, Juliet's House. While the historical accuracy of the connection to Shakespeare's play is debatable, the iconic balcony remains a popular attraction. Touch the bronze statue of Juliet for good luck in love, or simply soak in the atmosphere of this romantic landmark.

Veronetta

1. A Walk Through Time: From Humble Beginnings to the Artistic Hub

- A Working-Class Past: Veronetta's history stretches back to Roman times, though its most defining period was during the Middle Ages and Renaissance. The area housed artisans, millers, and laborers, who played a vital role in the city's development. Evidence of this past can be seen in the simple yet sturdy buildings and narrow alleyways.

- A Bohemian Renaissance: In recent decades, Veronetta has undergone a remarkable transformation. Artists, attracted by affordable rents and a creative atmosphere, have revitalized the area. Former workshops have morphed into trendy bars and art galleries, while charming piazzas now host lively street markets.

• A Fusion of Styles: Veronetta's architecture reflects its diverse history. You'll find remnants of medieval towers alongside brightly colored facades of renovated buildings. Street art adds splashes of urban energy to the historical backdrop, creating a unique and captivating visual landscape.

2. A Feast for the Senses: Unveiling Veronetta's Delights

• A Paradise for Foodies with a Twist: Veronetta offers a culinary scene distinct from the traditional trattorias of the Centro Storico. Trendy cafes serving brunch and craft coffee mingle with innovative gastropubs and ethnic restaurants. Don't miss the chance to savor local craft beers at a microbrewery or indulge in delicious street food at a bustling market.

• A Boho Chic Shopping Experience: Forget the big-name brands – Veronetta is all about independent shops and hidden gems. Browse through vintage clothing stores overflowing with unique finds, discover locally crafted jewelry and artwork, or explore bookstores specializing in niche interests. Here, shopping becomes an adventure in uncovering hidden treasures.

- A Lively Nightscape: As the sun sets, Veronetta transforms into a vibrant hub for nightlife. Trendy bars with outdoor seating spill onto cobbled streets, live music spills from hidden venues, and youthful energy fills the air. Whether you're seeking a romantic aperitivo or a night of dancing, Veronetta offers something for everyone.

3. Beyond the Main Streets: Unveiling Hidden Gems

- Castelvecchio Bridge at Night: Stroll across the Ponte Scaligero (Castelvecchio Bridge) at night and admire Veronetta's skyline bathed in a warm glow. The illuminated bridge and the twinkling lights of the neighborhood create a magical atmosphere.

- Giardino Giusti: Escape the urban buzz and seek refuge in the Giardino Giusti, a stunning Renaissance garden located on the border of Veronetta. Explore its manicured lawns, hidden grottoes, and enjoy breathtaking views of the city.

- Teatro Nuovo: Veronetta boasts its own theater, the Teatro Nuovo. Catch a performance of contemporary drama, ballet, or even an opera for a taste of Veronese culture beyond the mainstream.

Borgo Trento

1. A Green Escape: Parks and Gardens Abound

• Giardino Giusti: Bordering Borgo Trento is the crown jewel—the Giardino Giusti. This meticulously manicured Renaissance garden offers a haven of tranquility. Explore its symmetrical pathways, hidden grottoes adorned with statues, and cypress hedges that frame breathtaking views of the city below.

• Parco delle Mura: Borgo Trento boasts the Parco delle Mura, a sprawling green area built on the remains of Verona's medieval city walls. This urban park offers walking and jogging paths, picnic areas, and playgrounds, making it a popular spot for families and locals seeking outdoor recreation.

• Colle San Pietro: For the more adventurous, a hike up Colle San Pietro Hill rewards you with panoramic vistas of Verona and the surrounding countryside. Explore the trails that wind through vineyards and olive groves, and enjoy the serenity of nature within the city limits.

2. A Family-Friendly Haven: Activities and Entertainment

- Verona Zoo: A delightful outing for families with young children is the Verona Zoo (Giardino Zoologico). Home to a diverse collection of animals from around the world, the zoo provides a fun and educational experience for visitors of all ages.

- Museo Napoleonico: History buffs can delve into the Napoleonic era at the Museo Napoleonico. Housed in a former monastery, the museum showcases artifacts, uniforms, and documents related to Napoleon's reign in Italy.

- Local Festivals and Events: Throughout the year, Borgo Trento comes alive with local festivals and events. From food fairs showcasing regional delicacies to open-air concerts held in the park, there's always something to experience and enjoy.

3. A Neighborhood Steeped in History: A Glimpse into the Past

- Roman Amphitheatre: Though not as grand as the Arena, the Borgo Trento Roman Amphitheatre offers a fascinating glimpse into the city's ancient past. Partially unearthed and undergoing restoration, the amphitheatre hints at the entertainment culture of Roman Verona.

• Castel San Pietro: Atop Colle San Pietro stand the ruins of Castel San Pietro, a medieval fortress that once served as a defensive outpost. Explore the remaining walls and imagine the soldiers who manned this strategic point, offering a glimpse into Verona's turbulent past.

• Hidden Churches: Dotted throughout Borgo Trento are charming little churches, each with its own unique history and architecture. Seek out the Chiesa di San Lorenzo, a Romanesque church with a beautiful bell tower, or the Chiesa di Santa Maria in Stelle, known for its 15th-century frescoes.

San Zeno District

1. A Journey Through Time: From Humble Beginnings to Religious Hub

• A Saint's Legacy: The San Zeno district's story revolves around its namesake, Saint Zeno, the patron saint of Verona. Legend has it that he built the first church on the site in the 4th century. The present Basilica di San Zeno, however, was constructed between the 10th and 12th centuries, showcasing the peak of Romanesque architecture in Northern Italy.

• A Medieval Tapestry: As you explore the San Zeno district, step back in time to Verona's medieval period. Narrow streets lined with colorful houses, remnants of ancient city walls, and the occasional hidden courtyard whisper tales of bygone eras. Imagine pilgrims making their way to the basilica, artisans plying their trades, and a vibrant community flourishing within these walls.

• A Modern Transformation: While retaining its historical charm, the San Zeno district has embraced modern life. Quaint cafes with outdoor seating offer respite from sightseeing, while trendy shops selling local crafts and artisan products cater to modern tastes. This harmonious blend of old and new creates a unique and inviting atmosphere.

2. A Feast for the Senses: Unveiling San Zeno's Delights

• A Culinary Adventure Around Every Corner: The San Zeno district boasts a diverse culinary scene. Indulge in traditional Veronese cuisine at a family-run trattoria, savor a delicious pizza at a lively pizzeria, or grab a quick bite at a local bakery. Don't miss the chance to try local wines like Valpolicella or Bardolino at a cozy enoteca (wine bar).

- Aromatherapy on the Streets: As you stroll through the San Zeno district, enticing aromas waft from hidden alleyways. The scent of freshly baked bread from a local bakery mingles with the rich aroma of cured meats and the sweet fragrance of roasting coffee beans, creating a symphony of delicious smells.

- A Visual Feast in Every Piazza: Each piazza in the San Zeno district offers a unique visual experience. Piazza San Zeno, the central square, is dominated by the imposing facade of the basilica. Piazza Corrubbio, brimming with cafes and shops, bustles with life, while smaller piazzas offer hidden oases of tranquility.

3. Beyond the Basilica: Unveiling Hidden Gems

- Museo Lapidario Maffeiano: Delve deeper into Verona's Roman past at the Museo Lapidario Maffeiano. This museum houses a collection of Roman sculptures, inscriptions, and artifacts, offering a glimpse into the city's early days.

- Porta San Zeno: Step back in time at Porta San Zeno, one of the last remaining medieval gateways to Verona.

Imagine its defensive role in protecting the city, and marvel at its architectural details.

- Santuario della Madonna di Lourdes: Seek solace at the Santuario della Madonna di Lourdes, a replica of the famous French pilgrimage site. This peaceful sanctuary offers a haven for prayer and reflection.

Chapter 9: Outdoor Activities and Day Trips

Giusti Gardens

1. A Walk Through Time: From Humble Beginnings to Ornamental Splendor

- A Family Legacy: The Giusti Gardens' story begins in the 15th century, when the Giusti family, originally from Tuscany, acquired the land. Initially used for dyeing wool, the plot was transformed into a garden by Agostino Giusti in the late 16th century. He envisioned it as a scenographic extension of the Giusti Palace, offering a series of terraces that gradually revealed the city's beauty.

- Renaissance Ideals on Display: The Giusti Gardens embody the principles of Renaissance garden design. Symmetry reigns supreme, with geometrically shaped flowerbeds, cypress avenues aligned with precision, and fountains positioned for maximum visual impact. Visitors are transported back to a time when order, beauty, and a connection with nature were paramount design principles.

• A Living Legacy: Remarkably, the Giusti Gardens have remained in the Giusti family for centuries. This enduring ownership has ensured the garden's meticulous preservation, allowing visitors to experience a genuine Renaissance masterpiece.

2. A Feast for the Senses: Unveiling the Garden's Delights

• A Visual Symphony: Beyond geometric perfection, the Giusti Gardens offer a vibrant tapestry of colors and textures. Immaculately clipped hedges in deep green hues contrast with vibrant seasonal blooms. Statues of mythological figures add pops of white against the backdrop of verdant foliage. Every corner offers a new visual composition, a testament to the garden's artistic design.

• Aromatic Encounters: As you stroll through the Giusti Gardens, subtle fragrances fill the air. Sweet-smelling roses and lavender mingle with the earthy scent of freshly turned soil and the crisp aroma of citrus trees.

This sensory experience adds another layer to the garden's charm.

• A Tranquil Escape: The Giusti Gardens offer a haven of peace and quiet in the heart of Verona. The gentle murmur of water fountains, the chirping of birds, and the rustling of leaves create a symphony of calming sounds. Escape the city's hustle and bustle and find serenity amidst the meticulously maintained flora.

3. Beyond the Manicured Lawns: Exploring Hidden Gems

• A Secret Grotto: Venture beyond the main pathways to discover a hidden grotto adorned with stalactites and stalagmites. This cool, damp haven offers a respite from the summer heat and a touch of mystery to the garden's overall design.

• A Breathtaking Vista: Climb to the highest terrace and be rewarded with a panoramic view of Verona. From this vantage point, admire the city's red-tiled rooftops, the majestic silhouette of the Arena, and the winding curves of the Adige River.

• A Whispering Past: The Giusti Gardens are more than just beautiful flora – they are a silent testament to the lives of those who walked their paths. Imagine the Giusti family strolling through the gardens, hosting social gatherings, or simply enjoying the serenity of their verdant oasis.

Parco delle Colombare

1. A Green Escape in the Heart of the City

• A Patch of Tranquility: Parco delle Colombare offers a welcome escape from the city's hustle and bustle. Mature trees provide shade on sunny days, while grassy areas beckon for picnics and relaxation. The gentle murmur of a small stream adds a touch of serenity to the park's atmosphere, making it a perfect spot for a peaceful break.

• A Playground for All Ages: The park caters to families with a dedicated playground featuring slides, swings, and climbing structures. Watch children's laughter fill the air as they burn off energy and create lasting memories. Even adults can find their inner child on the park's walking and jogging paths, perfect for a morning exercise routine or an evening stroll.

- A Haven for Wildlife: Parco delle Colombare serves as a vital green corridor for Verona's urban wildlife. Observe birds flitting through the trees, listen for the buzzing of bees, and appreciate the park's role in maintaining a healthy ecosystem within the city.

2. A Glimpse into Verona's Past: Unveiling Hidden Stories

- A Legacy of Wine Production: The park's name, "Colombare," translates to "dovecotes." Historically, these structures provided shelter for doves, whose droppings were used as natural fertilizer for vineyards. The presence of the Parco delle Colombare hints at a time when Verona's surrounding areas were dedicated to wine production, a tradition that continues to this day.

- Traces of Industrial Heritage: Another layer of history lies beneath the park's surface. The area was once home to a yellow clay quarry, a material used extensively in Veronese construction. While the quarry is no longer operational, its legacy lives on in the park's name and perhaps in the unique composition of the soil.

- A Place for Local Gatherings: Parco delle Colombare serves as a vital social hub for the surrounding neighborhoods. Observe local residents walking their dogs, families picnicking on weekends, and friends catching up on sunny afternoons. The park fosters a sense of community and provides a space for social interaction.

3. Beyond the Walking Paths: Exploring the Surroundings

• A Neighborhood Adventure: Venture beyond the park's boundaries and explore the surrounding neighborhoods. Discover charming cafes, hidden trattorias serving local cuisine, and unique shops selling Veronese specialties. Immersing yourself in local life offers a more authentic Veronese experience.

• A Historical Journey: A short walk from the park takes you to the San Giorgio neighborhood, known for its medieval churches and historical buildings. Explore the Basilica di San Giorgio in Braida, a 15th-century church with stunning frescoes, or delve deeper into Veronese history at the Museo Archeologico del Teatro Romano (Archaeological Museum of the Roman Theatre).

• A Taste of the Countryside: Despite its urban location, Parco delle Colombare offers a glimpse into the surrounding countryside. On a clear day, you can catch sight of rolling hills in the distance, a reminder of the region's rich agricultural heritage. This juxtaposition between city and nature adds to the park's unique charm.

Lake Garda Excursions

1. Sirmione and Lake Garda Cruise:

• A Journey Through Time and Beauty: Embark on a captivating journey to Sirmione, a charming peninsula town adorned with medieval Scaligero Castle, narrow cobbled streets, and captivating grottoes. Explore the town's historical landmarks, soak up the sunshine on the lakeside promenade, and indulge in a delicious lunch overlooking the sparkling blue waters.

• Cruise Across the Crystal-Clear Waters: After exploring the enchanting town of Sirmione, hop on a boat cruise for a unique perspective of Lake Garda. Glide across the crystal-clear waters, admire the majestic mountains that hug the shoreline, and capture breathtaking panoramic views.

• Scaligero Castle's Enthralling Legacy: Step back in time and explore the imposing Scaligero Castle, a 14th-century fortress that stands proudly at the entrance of Sirmione's harbor. Immerse yourself in the castle's rich history, climb the towers for panoramic vistas, and lose yourself in the captivating legends associated with this magnificent structure.

2. Verona, Sirmione, and Lake Garda Tour with Boat Cruise:

• Unveiling Verona's Treasures: Kick off your day by exploring Verona's captivating historical center. Witness the iconic Arena, a Roman amphitheater that continues to host world-renowned performances. Stroll through Piazza delle Erbe, a bustling market square brimming with fresh produce and local crafts. Don't forget to snap a photo at Juliet's balcony, a timeless symbol of love.

• A Picturesque Cruise on Lake Garda: Immerse yourself in the beauty of Lake Garda with a scenic boat cruise. As you sail across the crystal-clear waters, admire the charming towns dotting the shoreline, the lush green hills embracing the lake, and the majestic mountains rising in the distance.

- Sirmione's Enchanting Embrace: Disembark at Sirmione and embark on a captivating exploration of this enchanting town. Wander through narrow, cobbled streets lined with colorful houses, discover hidden piazzas, and treat yourself to a delicious meal overlooking the lake.

3. Explore Bardolino Wine Country with a Boat Tour and Lunch

- A Cruise Among Vineyards: Embark on a unique journey that combines the beauty of Lake Garda with the charm of Bardolino wine country. Take a scenic boat cruise across the lake, admiring the breathtaking scenery and the quaint towns nestled along the shoreline.

- Wine Tasting Extravaganza: Disembark and delve into the world of Bardolino wines. Visit a local winery, learn about the winemaking process from passionate producers, and tantalize your taste buds with tastings of renowned Bardolino varieties.

- A Delicious Lakeside Lunch: Indulge in a delightful lunch overlooking the picturesque landscape of Lake Garda. Savor fresh local cuisine paired with exquisite

Bardolino wines, creating a memorable culinary experience.

4. Private Garda and Limone Tour with Boat Cruise

- Tailor-Made Exploration: Experience the best of Lake Garda on a private tour crafted to your interests. Explore the charming town of Limone, renowned for its picturesque harbor, lemon groves, and quaint shops.

- A Boat Cruise with a Difference: Hop on a private boat cruise and discover hidden coves, secret beaches, and breathtaking natural landscapes inaccessible by land. Take a refreshing dip in the crystal-clear waters, soak up the sunshine on the deck, and create unforgettable memories on Lake Garda.

- Hidden Gems Unveiled: With a private tour guide, you'll have the advantage of venturing beyond the usual tourist spots. Discover hidden gems, charming villages, and breathtaking viewpoints that most visitors miss.

Valpolicella Wine Region

1. A Land Steeped in History: A Legacy of Winemaking

• Ancient Roots: The history of Valpolicella's viticulture stretches back centuries. Evidence suggests that grapes were cultivated here as early as the Etruscan and Rhaetian civilizations, with wine production flourishing during the Roman era. The name "Valpolicella" itself is thought to derive from the Latin "Vallis Policellae," meaning "Valley of Many Cellars," a testament to the region's longstanding dedication to winemaking.

• A Legacy of Passion: Grape cultivation and wine production have been woven into the very fabric of Valpolicella's identity for generations. Family-run wineries have passed down traditional techniques and a deep respect for the terroir, ensuring the continued excellence of Valpolicella wines.

• Denominazione di Origine Controllata (DOC): In 1968, Valpolicella was awarded the prestigious Denominazione di Origine Controllata (DOC) status, a designation that guarantees the authenticity and quality of wines produced within the region. This recognition further solidified Valpolicella's reputation as a leading producer of world-class wines.

2. A Spectrum of Delights: Exploring Valpolicella's Wines

• Valpolicella Classico and Valpolicella Superiore: The foundation of Valpolicella's production lies in these two DOC wines. Classico, characterized by its fresh and fruity profile, is a versatile red wine perfect for everyday enjoyment. Superiore, aged for a longer period, boasts a richer and more complex flavor profile.

• Ripasso: This unique wine undergoes a second fermentation process on the dried grape skins, or "ripasso," used for Amarone production. This results in a fuller-bodied and more intense expression of Valpolicella, offering a distinctive taste experience.

• The Crown Jewel: Amarone, the king of Valpolicella wines, is a full-bodied, dry red wine produced using the Appassimento method. Here, grapes are dried on mats for several months, concentrating their sugars and flavors. The resulting wine is a powerhouse of intensity, with notes of dark fruit, spice, and chocolate, and a long, lingering finish.

3. A Journey for the Senses: Exploring Valpolicella Beyond the Wine

• A Tapestry of Landscapes: Venture beyond the vineyards and discover the beauty of Valpolicella's diverse landscapes. Explore the foothills of the Lessini Mountains, hike through serene valleys, or cycle along scenic routes, all while breathing in the fresh country air.

• Charming Villages: Dotted throughout Valpolicella are quaint villages waiting to be explored. Stroll through the narrow alleys of Sant'Ambrogio di Valpolicella, admire the architectural gems of Fumane, or delve into the rich history of Negrar, the heart of the Valpolicella wine region.

• A Culinary Experience: Valpolicella's culinary scene offers a delightful union of fresh local produce and traditional recipes. Savor dishes featuring homemade pasta, succulent grilled meats, and seasonal vegetables, all perfectly paired with a glass of Valpolicella wine.

4. Planning Your Valpolicella Adventure

• Wine Tasting Tours: Immerse yourself in the world of Valpolicella wines by embarking on a guided tour. Visit renowned wineries, learn about the winemaking process from passionate producers, and indulge in tastings of various Valpolicella varieties.

- Food and Wine Festivals: Throughout the year, Valpolicella comes alive with food and wine festivals. These events offer a wonderful opportunity to experience the region's culture, savor local delicacies, and celebrate the bounty of Valpolicella's vineyards.

- Embrace the Slow Life: Valpolicella is an invitation to slow down, savor the moment, and appreciate the simple pleasures in life. Find a charming agriturismo (farm stay) nestled amidst the vineyards, relax in the tranquil countryside, and reconnect with nature.

Chapter 10: Food and Drink

Dining in Verona

1. A Taste of Tradition: Trattorias and Osterias

• Trattoria Magic: The heart of Veronese dining lies in its trattorias—unpretentious, family-run establishments serving up regional specialties in a warm and welcoming atmosphere. Imagine checkered tablecloths, friendly service, and the aroma of simmering sauces wafting from the kitchen. These restaurants are perfect for experiencing authentic Veronese cuisine at its finest.

• Must-Try Dishes: Indulge in regional classics like "bigoli con l'anatra" (thick spaghetti with duck sauce), "risotto all'Amarone" (risotto cooked with Amarone wine), or "pastissada de caval" (horse meat stew) – a local specialty for the adventurous eater. Don't forget to leave room for dessert and savor a slice of "pandoro" (a light, yeasted sweet bread) or a scoop of "gelato" (Italian ice cream).

- Osteria Delights: Similar to trattorias, osterias offer a more casual dining experience with a focus on fresh, seasonal ingredients. These establishments often boast an extensive wine list, allowing you to pair your meal with the perfect local Valpolicella or Soave.

2. Fine Dining Delights: Modern Cuisine with a View

- A Touch of Modernity: While Verona cherishes its culinary traditions, a vibrant scene of modern restaurants is flourishing. These establishments take inspiration from global flavors while showcasing the finest local produce. Expect innovative dishes, stylish presentations, and impeccable service.

- Rooftop Restaurants: For a truly special dining experience, seek out Verona's rooftop restaurants. Imagine savoring a gourmet meal while gazing over the city's red-tiled rooftops, with the Arena di Verona as a breathtaking backdrop. These restaurants offer an unforgettable combination of culinary artistry and stunning views.

- Michelin-Starred Splendor: For the ultimate fine-dining experience, Verona boasts a handful of Michelin-starred restaurants. These establishments push the boundaries of culinary creativity, offering an explosion of flavors and textures presented with meticulous attention to detail.

3. Beyond the Restaurant Walls: Exploring Verona's Culinary Gems

• The Allure of Aperitivo: Embrace the Italian tradition of "aperitivo," an evening ritual involving drinks and small bites. Head to a bar or cafe in the late afternoon, sip on a refreshing Spritz or local wine, and enjoy a selection of appetizers ranging from olives and cured meats to mini pizzas and bruschetta.

• Verona's Food Markets: Immerse yourself in the sights, sounds, and smells of Verona's bustling food markets. Explore stalls overflowing with fresh produce, local cheeses, cured meats, and freshly baked bread. It's the perfect place to pick up ingredients for a picnic or to sample local specialties.

• Cooking Classes: Get hands-on with Veronese cuisine by enrolling in a cooking class. Learn from experienced chefs, master the art of making fresh pasta, and discover the secrets behind traditional dishes. This is a unique way to deepen your understanding of Veronese food culture.

Traditional Veronese Cuisine

1. A Land of Plenty: Setting the Stage for Culinary Delights

• Gifts from the Land: Verona's cuisine is deeply rooted in the fertile plains and rolling hills of the surrounding region. Fresh ingredients like Vialone Nano rice, a prized local variety known for its creamy texture, and seasonal vegetables like radicchio (red chicory) and asparagus form the foundation of many dishes.

• Wine Country Influence: Nestled amidst renowned wine regions like Valpolicella and Soave, Verona's cuisine is naturally influenced by these prestigious vintages. Expect to find wines incorporated into sauces, used for cooking risotto, and, of course, perfectly paired with every course.

• A Touch of History: Centuries of foreign rule, from the Scaligeri family to the Austrian Habsburgs, have left their mark on Veronese cuisine. Germanic influences can be seen in the use of hearty ingredients like sausages and cabbage, while Venetian techniques like breading and frying add another layer of flavor.

2. A Symphony of Flavors: Signature Dishes of Verona

- Bigoli con l'Anatra (Thick Spaghetti with Duck Sauce): This hearty dish showcases the robust flavors of the region. Thick, chewy bigoli pasta, similar to spaghetti, is bathed in a rich duck sauce, often featuring vegetables, and simmered to perfection. True Veronese comfort food.

- Risotto all'Amarone: A celebration of Verona's renowned wine, Amarone. This decadent risotto is cooked with amarone, infusing the rice with a deep, complex flavor profile. Parmigiano Reggiano cheese and a touch of butter add a creamy richness, making this dish a true star of Veronese cuisine.

- Gnocchi al Gorgonzola: These pillowy-soft potato gnocchi are a delightful expression of Veronese simplicity. Often served with a creamy gorgonzola cheese sauce and a sprinkle of walnuts, this dish offers a perfect balance of textures and flavors.

• Pastissada de Caval (Horse Meat Stew): a dish steeped in history and not for the faint of heart. Horse meat, slow-cooked with vegetables and red wine, creates a rich and flavorful stew. This traditional dish is a testament to Verona's resourceful culinary past.

3. Beyond the Classics: Hidden Gems of Veronese Cuisine

• Less is more: Antipasti (Starters): Veronese meals often begin with a selection of antipasti, showcasing the region's fresh produce and local specialties. Expect cured meats like Soppressa Veronese, pickled vegetables, bean salads, and small fried fish called "pesce persico."

• Lesso con la Pearà (Boiled Meat with Pearà Sauce): A quintessential Veronese dish, featuring boiled beef or veal with a unique pearà sauce. This rich and creamy sauce is made with breadcrumbs, broth, marrow, and cheese, offering a delightful counterpoint to the simplicity of the boiled meat.

• Verona's Sweet Endings: No Veronese meal is complete without a sweet finale. Savor a slice of "pandoro," a light and airy yeasted cake, perfect with a cup of espresso. For a touch of local flair, try "reziola," a sweet bread flavored with anise seeds.

4. A Taste of Tradition: Where to Find Veronese Cuisine

• Trattorias and Osterias: The heart and soul of Veronese dining lies in its trattorias and osterias. These family-run establishments offer a warm and welcoming atmosphere, with menus featuring regional specialties prepared using time-honored recipes.

• Agriturismos (Farm Stays): For a truly authentic experience, head to an agriturismo nestled amidst the rolling hills of the Veronese countryside. These farm stays often offer meals prepared using fresh, seasonal ingredients grown on their own land, showcasing the true essence of Veronese cuisine.

The Best Restaurants by Budget

1. Budget-Friendly Feasts (under €15 per person):

• Paninoteche: These sandwich shops are a lifesaver for budget-conscious travelers. Grab a fresh panini (Italian sandwich) overflowing with local meats, cheeses, and vegetables for a quick and satisfying meal. Look for local favorites like "soppressata" (salami) and "radicchio" (red chicory) on your panini.

• Pizza by the Slice: Forget fancy sit-down meals and head to a pizzeria for pizza "al taglio" (by the slice). Choose from a variety of toppings, grab a slice or two, and enjoy a casual and delicious lunch or dinner on the go. Keep an eye out for lunch deals at pizzerias, where you can often score a slice and a drink at a discounted price.

• Street Food: Verona's streets come alive with food vendors, especially during lunchtime. Look for vendors selling "arrosticini" (grilled skewers of meat), "panzerotti" (fried dough pockets filled with ricotta cheese and tomato sauce), and "calzone" (folded pizza filled with ricotta cheese and other ingredients). These affordable treats are perfect for a quick bite or a budget-friendly snack.

• Trattorias and Osterias: Don't be fooled by their unpretentious exterior. Trattorias and osterias are havens for delicious and affordable meals. Look for daily lunch specials ("menu del giorno") that often include a starter, a main course, and a glass of wine for a fixed price.

These are a great way to experience authentic Veronese cuisine without breaking the bank. Pro Tip: Head to these establishments for lunch, as they often offer more affordable options compared to dinner.

2. Mid-Range Delights (between €15 and €30 per person):

• Trattorias and Osterias (Full Menu): While trattorias and osterias offer budget-friendly lunch options, they truly shine with their full a la carte menus. Indulge in regional specialties like "bigoli con l'anatra" (thick spaghetti with duck sauce) or "risotto all'Amarone" (risotto cooked with Amarone wine) at a reasonable price. Don't forget to pair your meal with a glass of local Valpolicella or Soave wine for an even more authentic experience.

• Pasta Restaurants: Verona is a pasta paradise. Venture beyond tourist traps and seek out local pasta restaurants where you can savor fresh, homemade pasta dishes at reasonable prices. Explore options like "lasagne al ragù" (layered pasta with meat sauce) or "tagliatelle al tartufo" (pasta ribbons with truffle sauce) for a truly satisfying meal.

- Pizzerias (Sit-Down): Take your pizza experience a step further by enjoying a sit-down meal at a traditional pizzeria. These establishments offer a wider selection of pizzas compared to pizza-by-the slice shops. Choose from classic pizzas like "Margherita" or "Marinara" or explore pizzas with more creative toppings.

3. A Splurge for Special Occasions (above €30 per person):

- Fine-Dining Establishments: For a truly special occasion, Verona boasts a selection of fine-dining restaurants. These establishments offer an upscale dining experience with innovative dishes, impeccable service, and stunning ambiance. Expect to pay a premium for the experience, but be prepared for an unforgettable culinary journey.

- Rooftop Restaurants: Combine breathtaking views with a gourmet meal at one of Verona's rooftop restaurants. Imagine savoring exquisite dishes while gazing over the city's red-tiled rooftops, with the Arena di Verona as a backdrop. This is a splurge experience, perfect for a romantic evening or a celebratory dinner.

4. Beyond the Restaurant Walls: Saving Money While Eating Well

• Picnics in the Park: Verona boasts beautiful parks like Giardino Giusti and Parco delle Mura. Grab some fresh bread, cheese, cured meats, and seasonal fruits from the local market and enjoy a delightful and affordable picnic lunch amidst nature's beauty.

• Happy Hour: Many bars and cafes offer "happy hour" specials, with discounted drinks and appetizers. This is a great way to sample local wines and enjoy a pre-dinner bite without breaking the bank.

Street Food and Markets

1. Aromatic Delights: Unveiling Verona's Street Food Culture

• A Feast for the Senses: As you stroll through Verona's charming streets, be sure to follow the enticing aromas that waft from street vendors. These mobile kitchens offer a delectable array of quick bites, perfect for a light lunch, a satisfying snack, or a budget-friendly meal.

- A World of Flavors: Verona's street food scene is a melting pot of flavors. Indulge in classic Italian treats like "arancini" (fried rice balls filled with savory fillings), "suppli" (fried rice balls with mozzarella cheese), and "panzerotti" (fried dough pockets filled with ricotta cheese and tomato sauce).

- Local Specialties: For a taste of Verona, seek out vendors selling "arrosticini" (grilled skewers of lamb or sausage) – a local favorite. Don't miss the chance to try "folpetti al sugo" (octopus stew) or "bigoli con l'anatra" (thick spaghetti with duck sauce) in smaller portions from street vendors.

- Sweet Endings: No Italian adventure is complete without a sweet treat. Look for vendors selling "crepes" filled with Nutella, fresh fruit, or whipped cream. For a local option, try "sbrisolona," a crumbly cake made with cornmeal and almonds.

2. A Treasure Trove for Foodies: Exploring Verona's Markets

- Piazza delle Erbe: This bustling market square is the heart of Verona's food scene. Stalls overflow with fresh produce, from seasonal fruits and vegetables to local cheeses and cured meats. Sample local delicacies like "soppressata" (salami) and "Monte Baldo cheese" while soaking up the lively atmosphere.

• Pescheria (Fish Market): Head to the Pescheria for the freshest seafood in Verona. Marvel at the glistening displays of fish, shellfish, and crustaceans, and be tempted by the enticing aroma of freshly caught seafood sizzling on grills.

• Porta Borsari Market: This historic market, housed within the Porta Borsari city gate, offers a mix of local produce, souvenirs, and handcrafted goods. While not exclusively focused on food, you can still find vendors selling fresh bread, cured meats, and local honey.

3. Beyond the Food: Markets as Cultural Experiences

• A Glimpse into Local Life: Visiting Verona's markets is not just about the food; it's about experiencing the city's vibrant energy and connecting with the locals. Observe vendors passionately hawking their wares, barter for the best prices, and practice your Italian with friendly conversations.

• A Feast for the Eyes: The colorful displays of fresh produce, the glistening seafood counters, and the artistic presentations of cured meats are a visual treat. Be sure to capture the vibrant energy of the markets with your camera.

4. Tips for Navigating Verona's Street Food Scene and Markets

• Embrace Cash: While some vendors may accept cards, cash is still the preferred mode of payment at most street food stalls and markets. Come prepared with small bills for easier transactions.

• Seasonal Specialties: The beauty of street food lies in its seasonal offerings. Embrace the local bounty and ask vendors about their recommendations based on what's freshest at the time of your visit.

• Don't Be Shy: Don't hesitate to ask vendors questions about their offerings. Most will be happy to explain the ingredients and recommend the best choices for your taste.

Chapter 11: Wine and Nightlife

Wine Bars and Tastings

1. Beyond the Bottle: Exploring Verona's Wine Bars

- Enotecas: A Haven for Wine Lovers: Enotecas (wine bars) are the beating heart of Verona's wine scene. Imagine cozy, dimly lit spaces lined with shelves overflowing with local and international wines. These establishments offer a chance to sample a variety of wines by the glass, often paired with small plates of cheese, cured meats, and other delicious bites.

- A Local Experience: Verona's enotecas are more than just places to drink; they're social hubs where locals and visitors gather to unwind and connect over a glass of wine. Embrace the convivial atmosphere, strike up conversations with friendly staff, and let them guide you through the world of Veronese wines.

- Exploring Different Styles: Verona's wine bars cater to all palates. Seek out establishments specializing in regional wines like Valpolicella Classico, Amarone, and

Soave. For a wider selection, explore enotecas, which offer a diverse range of Italian and international wines.

2. A Sensory Experience: Unveiling Wine Tastings in Verona

• A Journey Through Valpolicella: Embark on a guided tour through the picturesque vineyards of Valpolicella. Learn about the region's unique grape varietals, the traditional winemaking methods, and the history behind iconic wines like Amarone. Culminate your experience with a tasting of various Valpolicella wines in a charming winery setting.

• Unveiling the Secrets of Winemaking: Delve deeper with a winemaking class. Learn the art of grape selection, crushing, fermentation, and aging. Many wineries offer interactive classes where you can participate in the process and gain a deeper appreciation for the winemaking craft.

• Private Tastings for Discerning Palates: For a truly personalized experience, consider a private wine tasting. Work with a local wine expert to curate a tasting based on your preferences, allowing you to explore specific varietals, vintage years, or regional specialties.

3. Beyond the Tasting Room: Pairing Wine with Food

• Wine Bars with Food Pairings: Many wine bars in Verona offer curated tasting experiences that pair specific wines with delicious food pairings. This allows you to not only appreciate the individual flavors of the wine but also experience how they complement different dishes.

• Wine and Dine at Local Restaurants: Verona boasts an abundance of restaurants that champion local wines. Pair your meal with a glass of Valpolicella or Soave, recommended by the knowledgeable staff, to create a perfect harmony of flavors and celebrate the culinary heritage of the region.

4. Planning Your Wine Adventure in Verona

• Consider the Season: Grape harvests typically occur in September. Visiting during this time allows you to witness the harvest firsthand and participate in special harvest-themed events at many wineries.

• Booking Tastings: Popular wineries often have limited availability for tours and tastings. Consider booking your experience in advance, especially during peak tourist season.

- Transportation Options: While some wineries are accessible by public transportation, renting a car or booking a guided tour with transportation included offers more flexibility for exploring the vineyards of Valpolicella.

The Best Nightlife Spots

1. A Night of Conversation and Craft Brews: Lively Bars and Pubs

- Caffè Filippini: Established in 1901, this historic cafe is a local institution. While not strictly a nighttime venue, Caffè Filippini transforms into a lively bar in the evenings. Mingle with Veronese locals, sip on a craft beer, and soak up the city's vibrant atmosphere.
- M27: This trendy spot is a haven for Verona's young and hip crowd. Expect a cool, modern ambiance, a wide selection of craft beers on tap, and upbeat music that encourages conversation and socializing.
- Celtic Pub Verona: A touch of Ireland in the heart of Verona, the Celtic Pub offers a warm and welcoming atmosphere. Enjoy a pint of Guinness, watch live sports

on the big screen, and engage in friendly banter with fellow patrons.

• Santa Maria Craft Pub: This pub is a paradise for craft beer enthusiasts. Boasting an extensive selection of local and international brews on tap, Santa Maria offers a relaxed setting to unwind and savor a variety of flavors.

2. A Night of Class and Cocktails: Sophisticated Lounges and Bars

• The Soda Jerk: Hidden away in a historic building, The Soda Jerk offers a unique and upscale cocktail experience. Expert bartenders craft innovative cocktails using fresh ingredients and premium spirits. The intimate atmosphere and stylish decor create a perfect spot for a romantic evening or a night out with friends.

• Archivio: This bar is a haven for those who appreciate the art of mixology. Expert bartenders create classic cocktails with a twist, alongside innovative concoctions that will tantalize your taste buds. The elegant setting and attentive service make Archivio an ideal spot for a sophisticated night out.

• Dorian Gray: This bar combines a restaurant and a nightclub, offering a versatile experience. Start your evening with a delicious meal, then transition to the stylish bar area for expertly crafted cocktails and a sophisticated ambiance.

3. A Night of Dancing and DJs: Energetic Clubs and Discos

• Alter Ego: Considered Verona's most popular club, Alter Ego boasts a spacious dance floor, a state-of-the-art sound system, and resident DJs spinning the latest hits. Prepare to dance the night away in this energetic and trendy atmosphere.

• Hollywood Dance Club: This club caters to fans of popular music and international DJs. Expect a vibrant crowd, a lively atmosphere, and a chance to dance the night away to your favorite tunes.

• Berfi's Club: Located in the heart of Verona, Berfi's Club offers a more intimate clubbing experience. With a focus on electronic music and local DJs, this club attracts a dedicated following that comes for the energetic atmosphere and friendly crowd.

4. Beyond the Club Walls: Exploring Verona's Nightlife Gems

- Live Music: Verona boasts a thriving live music scene. Check local listings for bars and cafes hosting live music nights featuring everything from jazz and blues to local bands and up-and-coming artists.

- Opera Under the Stars: During the summer months, the Verona Arena transforms into a magical open-air opera venue. Experience the grandeur of opera under the starlit sky for a truly unforgettable evening.

- Piazza Bra Nights: The iconic Piazza Bra comes alive at night, with cafes and bars bustling with activity. Grab a drink, people-watch, and soak up the vibrant energy of the city after dark.

Cafes and Gelaterias

1. The Ritual of Coffee: Unveiling Verona's Cafe Culture

- Caffè al Banco (Coffee at the Bar): Immerse yourself in the local coffee culture by ordering a "caffè al banco" (coffee at the bar). Standing at the counter, sip your espresso quickly and efficiently—the perfect pick-me-up to start your day or a welcome break in between sightseeing.

• Pasticceria Delights: Many cafes are also pasticcerias (pastry shops). Pair your espresso with a flaky cornetto (Italian croissant), a decadent sfogliatella (ricotta-filled pastry), or a slice of "torta della nonna" (grandmother's cake) for a truly satisfying breakfast or afternoon treat.

• Historic Cafes: Verona boasts historic cafes that have been serving locals and visitors for generations. Places like Caffè Borsari and Caffè Dante offer a timeless ambiance and a chance to soak up the city's rich history while enjoying a cup of coffee.

2. A World of Gelato: Unveiling Verona's Finest Ice Cream

• Artisanal Gelato: Verona takes its gelato seriously. Forget the mass-produced varieties; here, the focus is on artisanal gelato, made with fresh, high-quality ingredients and churned daily.

• A Symphony of Flavors: Verona's gelaterias offer a seemingly endless selection of flavors, from classic favorites like chocolate and pistachio to more unique options like lavender honey or ricotta fig. Don't be afraid to ask for samples to find your perfect flavor combination.

- The Art of the Passeggiata: Indulging in gelato is often part of the "passeggiata" (evening stroll) in Verona. Grab a cone or cup and join the locals as they leisurely stroll through the charming streets, savoring their gelato and enjoying the cool evening air.

3. Beyond the Classics: Unveiling Unique Cafes and Gelaterias

- Specialty Coffee Shops: For coffee connoisseurs, Verona offers specialty coffee shops with a focus on single-origin beans, slow brewing methods, and expertly crafted latte art.

- Vegan and Gluten-Free Options: Verona caters to dietary restrictions as well. Several cafes and gelaterias offer vegan pastries and dairy-free or gluten-free gelato options, ensuring everyone can enjoy a delicious treat.

- Gelato with a View: For a truly special experience, head to a gelateria with a view. Imagine savoring your gelato while overlooking the iconic Piazza Bra or the enchanting Ponte Pietra bridge.

4. Tips for Navigating Verona's Cafes and Gelaterias

- Cash is King: While some cafes and gelaterias accept cards, cash is still the preferred mode of payment at many establishments. Come prepared with small bills for easier transactions.

• Seasonal Specialties: Just like with street food, gelaterias often feature seasonal flavors made with fresh, local ingredients. Embrace the changing offerings and try something new based on what's in season during your visit.

• The Art of Ordering: When ordering gelato, you can choose a "cono" (cone) or a "coppetta" (cup). For multiple flavors, consider a "coppetta" to prevent messy drips!

Chapter 12: Shopping and Souvenirs

Local Markets and Boutiques

1. A Feast for the Senses: Exploring Verona's Local Markets

• Piazza delle Erbe: This lively square is the heart of Verona's market scene. Every weekday morning, the piazza transforms into a bustling marketplace. Stalls overflow with fresh fruits and vegetables, fragrant local cheeses, cured meats, and an array of colorful flowers. Immerse yourself in the sights, sounds, and aromas as you browse the offerings and soak up the lively atmosphere.

• Porta Borsari Market: Housed within the historic Porta Borsari city gate, this market offers a mix of local produce, souvenirs, and handcrafted goods. While not exclusively focused on food, you can still find vendors selling fresh bread, cured meats, and local honey. Be sure to admire the impressive architecture of the gate while you browse the market stalls.

- Mercato del Sabato (Saturday Market): Head to the Borgo Trento neighborhood for the Saturday Market. This local market offers a chance to find unique treasures alongside everyday essentials. Expect to find clothing, household goods, antiques, and, of course, fresh produce from local farms.

- Flea Markets: Verona boasts occasional flea markets, particularly on the third Saturday of the month at Piazza San Zeno. These markets are a treasure trove for vintage clothing enthusiasts, antique collectors, and anyone seeking unique finds.

2. A Treasure Trove for Fashionistas: Unveiling Verona's Boutiques

- Via Mazzini: This pedestrianized street is Verona's answer to a luxury shopping haven. Lined with designer boutiques showcasing international brands like Gucci, Prada, and Louis Vuitton, Via Mazzini is perfect for those seeking high-end fashion finds.

- Corso Porta Borsari: This charming cobbled street offers a mix of established Italian brands and independent boutiques. Expect to find quality clothing, shoes, and accessories at a slightly more affordable price range compared to Via Mazzini.

• Hidden Gems: Verona boasts a delightful selection of independent shops tucked away on charming side streets. Explore these hidden gems to discover unique handcrafted jewelry, locally designed clothing lines, and specialty shops selling everything from leather goods to artisan chocolates.

• Souvenir Shops: For a piece of Verona to take home, browse the souvenir shops around the city center. Find everything from classic postcards and fridge magnets to locally-made crafts, glassware featuring Verona's landmarks, and bottles of Valpolicella wine.

3. Beyond the Shopping Bags: Tips for Navigating Verona's Shopping Scene

• Bargaining: While not as common as in some other countries, a little friendly bargaining is sometimes possible, particularly at flea markets and antique shops.

• Opening Hours: Most shops in Verona typically follow standard Italian opening hours, closed for a midday break between 1:00 pm and 4:00 pm. On Sundays, many shops are closed entirely, with the exception of souvenir shops in tourist areas.

• Tax Refunds: Tourists who are not residents of the European Union may be eligible for a VAT (value-added tax) refund on purchases. Be sure to inquire at the shop about tax-free shopping options.

Shopping Streets: Via Mazzini and Corso Porta Borsari

1. Via Mazzini: A Luxurious Playground

• A Haven for High-End Fashion: Via Mazzini is Verona's undisputed champion of luxury shopping. Imagine strolling down a pedestrianized street lined with elegant storefronts, each showcasing the latest collections from world-renowned designers. Expect to find flagship stores of iconic brands like Gucci, Prada, Louis Vuitton, and many more.

• A Feast for the Eyes: Window shopping on Via Mazzini is a treat in itself. The sleek displays, meticulously curated mannequins showcasing the latest trends, and the overall ambiance of luxury create a visually stunning experience.

- People-Watching Paradise: Via Mazzini is not just about shopping; it's a place to see and be seen. Observe stylish locals and well-heeled tourists browsing the stores, adding a touch of people-watching entertainment to your shopping spree.

2. Beyond the Big Brands: A Hidden Gem or Two

- Independent Boutiques: While Via Mazzini is dominated by luxury brands, a few hidden gems cater to those seeking something unique. Tucked away amidst the designer stores, you might find an independent boutique specializing in high-end Italian-made shoes or a local jewelry designer showcasing exquisite handcrafted pieces. Keep your eyes peeled for these treasures!

- Department Stores: For a wider selection of brands under one roof, head to La Rinascente, a prestigious Italian department store located on Via Mazzini. Here, you'll find a curated mix of designer and contemporary labels alongside beauty counters, homeware departments, and more.

3. Planning Your Shopping Spree on Via Mazzini

- Budget Considerations: Window shopping is free, but be prepared for sticker shock if you plan on indulging in designer purchases. Via Mazzini caters to high-end tastes and carries hefty price tags. Consider setting a budget beforehand and sticking to it.

- Opening Hours: Most stores on Via Mazzini typically follow standard Italian opening hours, with a midday break between 1:00 p.m. and 4:00 p.m.. On Sundays, most shops are closed entirely.

- Tax Refunds: Tourists who are not residents of the European Union may be eligible for a VAT (value-added tax) refund on purchases. Inquire at the store about tax-free shopping options.

4. Corso Porta Borsari: A Charming Mix

- A Blend of Established Brands and Local Boutiques: Corso Porta Borsari offers a more relaxed and affordable shopping experience compared to Via Mazzini. This charming cobbled street is lined with a delightful mix of established Italian brands like Max Mara and Brunello Cucinelli, alongside independent boutiques showcasing local designers and trendy labels.

- Quality at a Fair Price: Corso Porta Borsari is a great place to find high-quality clothing, shoes, and accessories at a more accessible price range compared to Via Mazzini. Here, you can find well-made Italian staples and trendy pieces without breaking the bank.

- A Local Vibe: Corso Porta Borsari offers a more authentic Veronese shopping experience. Expect a slower pace, friendly shopkeepers, and the opportunity to discover unique finds from local designers and artisans.

5. A Treasure Trove Beyond Clothing:

Specialty Shops: While clothing stores dominate Corso Porta Borsari, you'll also find specialty shops selling everything from leather goods and handcrafted jewelry to homewares and gourmet food stores. Take some time to explore these unique shops and discover hidden treasures.

6. Planning Your Shopping Spree on Corso Porta Borsari

- Bargaining: While not as common as in some other countries, a little friendly bargaining is sometimes possible, particularly at smaller independent shops. Don't be afraid to politely inquire about a discount, especially if you're buying multiple items.

• Opening Hours: Similar to Via Mazzini, most shops on Corso Porta Borsari follow standard Italian opening hours with a midday break. On Sundays, expect many shops to be closed.

• A Relaxing Experience: Corso Porta Borsari offers a more laid-back shopping experience compared to the fast-paced luxury of Via Mazzini. Take your time, browse at your leisure, and soak up the charming atmosphere of this delightful street.

Specialty Shops: Olive Oil, Wine, and More

1. Liquid Gold: Unveiling Verona's Olive Oil Delights

• Frantoio Ranzenigo: Nestled in the heart of Valpolicella, this historic olive mill offers a unique experience. Witness the traditional olive oil production process and indulge in a tasting of their award-winning extra virgin olive oil. Choose from delicate monovarietal oils to robust blends, each capturing the essence of the Valpolicella region.

• Specialty Food Stores: Many gourmet food stores in Verona stock a wide selection of high-quality olive oils from various regions of Italy. These shops often have knowledgeable staff who can guide you through the different varieties and recommend the perfect oil to complement your favorite dishes.

• Markets: The bustling markets of Verona, like Piazza delle Erbe, often feature stalls selling local olive oil. Engage with the vendors, sample their offerings, and discover unique small-batch olive oils produced by local farmers.

2. A Journey Through the Vine: Unveiling Verona's Wine Shops

• Enotecas (Wine Bars): These establishments are more than just places to enjoy a glass of wine; they often double as shops selling a curated selection of local and regional wines. Enotecas like La Cantina di Romeo or Enoteca Custoza offer expert recommendations and allow you to purchase bottles to take home.

- Wineries: For a truly immersive experience, venture out to the rolling hills of Valpolicella and visit a local winery. Many wineries offer tours, tastings, and the opportunity to purchase their wines directly from the source. Experience the passion of local winemakers and discover the unique characteristics of Valpolicella wines like Amarone and Recioto.

- Specialty Wine Shops: Verona boasts specialty wine shops like Divino Wine Pleasure or Enoteca Emporio di Vino. These shops offer an extensive selection of wines from different regions of Italy, with a strong focus on local and Valpolicella wines. Their knowledgeable staff can help you navigate the vast selection and find the perfect bottle for your taste and budget.

3. Beyond the Vine and Olive Grove: Discovering Other Delights

- Cheese Shops: Verona boasts charming cheese shops like Caseificio Perini or La Bottega Casearia. These shops offer a delightful selection of local and regional cheeses, from creamy mozzarella to sharp pecorino. Sample different varieties, pair them with a glass of wine, and discover the rich cheesemaking traditions of Italy.

- Salumerie (Cured Meat Shops): No Italian culinary experience is complete without cured meats. Salumerie like Salumeria Mastrotto or G. Boninsegna Salumeria offer an array of cured meats like prosciutto, salami, and speck. Sample different varieties, indulge in a "panino" (sandwich) filled with cured meats and cheese, and stock up on these delicious savory treats to take home.

- Chocolate Shops: Verona has a sweet tooth, and chocolate shops like Bottega Coletti or Giambattista Modì offer a delightful indulgence. Discover decadent truffles, hand-crafted chocolates with unique flavors, and beautifully wrapped boxes perfect for souvenirs.

4. Tips for Navigating Verona's Specialty Shops

- Embrace the Language: A few Italian phrases like "vorrei assaggiare" (I would like to taste) or "posso avere un consiglio?" (Can I have a recommendation?) can go a long way in enhancing your shopping experience. Most shopkeepers will appreciate your effort.

- Don't Be Afraid to Ask: The staff at specialty shops are passionate about their products and knowledgeable about local offerings. Ask questions, sample different varieties, and let them guide you towards the perfect purchase.

• Consider Shipping Options: Some specialty shops offer shipping options, allowing you to take home larger quantities of olive oil, wine, or other products without having to worry about carrying them in your luggage.

Chapter 13: Events and Festivals

Annual Events

1. Springtime Celebrations

• Verona in Love (February): As the name suggests, Verona truly embraces love in February. The city transforms into a romantic haven with special events, themed decorations, and Valentine's Day celebrations that go beyond the ordinary.

• Vinitaly (March): This prestigious event is the world's largest wine and oenology fair. Held annually in Verona, Vinitaly attracts wine producers, distributors, and enthusiasts from all over the globe. Even if you're not a wine expert, the sheer scale and energy of the event are impressive.

2. Summer Spectacles

• Verona Opera Festival (June–September): Experience the magic of opera under the stars at the Verona Arena, a spectacular Roman amphitheater. The festival attracts world-renowned opera singers and orchestras, creating an unforgettable experience for opera lovers.

- Tocatì—International Festival of Street Games (September): This playful event transforms Verona's streets into a giant game board. Witness traditional and new games come to life, participate in workshops, and rediscover the joy of simple pleasures with locals and visitors alike.

3. Autumn Delights

- FieraCavalli (Horse Fair) (October): Verona's equestrian tradition comes alive at the FieraCavalli. This prestigious event showcases horse breeds from around the world, features equestrian competitions, and offers a chance to immerse yourself in the world of horses.

- Christmas Markets in Verona (December): Verona transforms into a winter wonderland during the festive season. Enchanting Christmas markets fill the squares with twinkling lights, festive decorations, and an array of local crafts, delicious treats, and heartwarming Christmas cheer.

4. Beyond the Big Events: Unveiling Hidden Gems

- Local Festivals: Throughout the year, Verona's neighborhoods come alive with local festivals celebrating patron saints, harvest seasons, or specific traditions. These smaller events offer a glimpse into the local culture and a chance to connect with the Veronese community.

- Concerts and Performances: Verona boasts a vibrant cultural scene with year-round concerts, theater performances, and art exhibitions. Check local listings for events happening during your visit and discover hidden gems beyond the major festivals.

5. Planning Your Verona Experience with Events in Mind

- Consider the Season: Verona's events are spread throughout the year, making it a year-round destination. If you have a particular event in mind, plan your trip accordingly to ensure you don't miss it.

- Accommodation: Popular events like the Verona Opera Festival can lead to higher hotel rates and limited availability.

- Embrace the Spirit: Verona's events are more than just spectator experiences. Participate in workshops, join the crowds for lively celebrations, and soak up the infectious energy of the city during these festive occasions.

Verona Opera Festival

1. A Stage Steeped in History: The Allure of the Arena

• A Roman Amphitheater Reborn: The heart of the festival is the Verona Arena, a spectacular Roman amphitheater built in the 1st century AD. Imagine witnessing grand operas performed on the same stage that once hosted gladiatorial contests and chariot races. The open-air setting and the Arena's impressive acoustics create a truly unique and magical atmosphere.

• A Legacy of Operatic Excellence: The Verona Arena Opera Festival has been a cultural cornerstone since 1913. Over the years, legendary singers like Luciano Pavarotti and Maria Callas have graced the stage, solidifying the festival's reputation as a premier opera destination.

2. A Season of Spectacle: Unveiling the Festival Program

- A Stellar Repertoire: The festival typically runs from June to September, showcasing a selection of classic and beloved operas. Expect to see masterpieces like Verdi's Aida and La Traviata, Puccini's Tosca and Madama Butterfly, and many more.

- World-Renowned Artists: The festival attracts internationally acclaimed opera singers, directors, and orchestras, ensuring a high caliber of performances. Witness the magic unfold as talented artists bring these timeless operas to life under the Verona sky.

- Something for Everyone: While the core audience comprises opera aficionados, the festival also caters to newcomers. Special events, introductory talks, and behind-the-scenes tours provide a deeper understanding of opera and enhance the overall experience.

3. Planning Your Arena Experience: Tips and Considerations

- Booking Tickets: Tickets for the Verona Opera Festival tend to sell out quickly. Plan your trip well in advance, and book your tickets online as soon as they become available. Consider different seating categories based on your budget and preference for proximity to the stage.

- Dress Code: While there's no strict dress code, the atmosphere leans towards smart casual or semi-formal attire. Pack comfortable yet stylish clothing suitable for outdoor summer evenings. Don't forget a light jacket or shawl for cooler nights.

- Weather Considerations: Verona summers can be quite warm. Opt for breathable fabrics, and bring sunscreen and a hat for protection during the day. Be prepared for occasional rain showers; a small umbrella or raincoat is recommended.

- Enhancing the Experience: Consider arriving early to soak up the pre-show atmosphere and explore the historic arena. Many restaurants in Verona offer special pre-opera menus, allowing you to enjoy a delicious meal before the performance.

4. Beyond the Stage: Unveiling the Festival's Fringe

- Citywide Buzz: During the festival, Verona pulsates with operatic energy. Expect street performances, themed exhibitions, and opera-inspired events throughout the city. Immerse yourself in the city-wide celebration of music and theater.

- Guided Tours: Several tour companies offer guided tours of the Arena, providing historical insights and a glimpse behind the scenes of the festival. Learn about the stage machinery, costume design, and the history of opera in Verona.

- Post-Performance Delights: After the curtain falls, extend the magic with a delicious dinner at a charming Veronese restaurant. Many restaurants offer special post-opera menus, allowing you to continue the conversation and relive the highlights of the performance.

Vinitaly Wine Fair

1. A Celebration of Winemaking Excellence

- A Global Gathering: Vinitaly is a magnet for winemakers, distributors, industry professionals, and passionate consumers from all over the world. It's a unique opportunity to connect with the who's who of the wine world, discover new varietals, and expand your knowledge of wine.

• A Showcase of Italian Wines: As the birthplace of iconic wines like Barolo, Brunello di Montalcino, and Amarone, Italy takes center stage at Vinitaly. Explore diverse regions, meet passionate producers, and sample a mind-boggling array of Italian wines.

• Beyond Italy's Borders: While Italy reigns supreme, Vinitaly also features a significant international presence. Discover wines from emerging regions, established countries, and hidden gems from around the globe.

2. A Multi-Sensory Experience: Unveiling the Delights of Vinitaly

• Wine Tastings Galore: The heart of Vinitaly lies in the countless tasting opportunities. Explore exhibition stands, attend masterclasses led by renowned wine experts, and embark on a journey of discovery through the diverse world of wine.

• Culinary Delights: Food and wine go hand in hand. Vinitaly features a plethora of food stands offering regional specialties perfectly paired with the wines being showcased. Indulge in delicious pairings and discover how food elevates the wine experience.

• Educational Opportunities: Vinitaly isn't just about tasting; it's about learning. The fair features a robust program of seminars, workshops, and conferences led by industry experts. Expand your wine knowledge, explore new trends, and gain valuable insights from the masters.

3. Planning Your Vinitaly Experience: Tips and Considerations

• Tickets and Registration: Tickets for Vinitaly are available online in advance. Consider registering for specific events or masterclasses that interest you, as space can be limited.

• Plan Your Itinerary: With thousands of exhibitors spread across vast exhibition halls, planning your visit is crucial. Identify producers or regions you're interested in beforehand and prioritize your exploration.

• Comfortable Clothing and Footwear: Vinitaly is a sprawling event, so comfortable shoes are essential. Dress in layers, as the temperature inside the exhibition halls can vary.

- Bring Your Business Cards: If you're a wine professional or aim to network with industry contacts, bring plenty of business cards to facilitate introductions and connections.

- Embrace the Language: A few basic Italian phrases like "posso assaggiare questo vino?" (can I taste this wine?) or "grazie" (thank you) will go a long way in enhancing your experience and showing respect to the producers.

Christmas Markets

1. A Feast for the Senses: Exploring Verona's Christmas Markets

- Piazza dei Signori: The heart of the Christmas market scene lies in Piazza dei Signori, also known as Piazza Dante. Imagine strolling through a fairytale landscape adorned with twinkling lights and overflowing with traditional wooden chalets. These charming stalls offer a treasure trove of Christmas delights.

- The Courtyard of the Old Market (Cortile del Mercato Vecchio): This historic square, adjacent to Piazza delle

Erbe, boasts a traditional Christmas market with a focus on local products. Find stalls brimming with delicious regional specialties, handmade crafts from local artisans, and unique Christmas decorations crafted by Veronese workshops.

• International Nativity Scene Festival: While not strictly a market, the annual Presepi Dal Mondo (International Nativity Scene Festival) held within the majestic Verona Arena is a delightful Christmas tradition. Witness a breathtaking display of nativity scenes from all over the world, showcasing artistic interpretations and breathtaking craftsmanship.

2. A Treasure Trove for Gift-Givers

• Handmade Crafts: Verona's Christmas markets are a haven for those seeking unique and locally-made gifts. Find handcrafted ornaments, beautifully embroidered linens, hand-painted ceramics, and exquisite jewelry, all imbued with Italian charm.

• Gourmet Delights: Indulge in the festive flavors of the season. Sample delectable local cheeses, cured meats, and sweet treats like panettone (a rich Italian Christmas cake) and torrone (a nougat candy). Stock up on gourmet food items like jams, honey, and olive oil to take a taste of Verona home with you.

• Festive Decorations: Bring the Christmas spirit home with handcrafted ornaments, twinkling lights, and unique nativity scene figurines. The markets offer a delightful selection of decorations to add a touch of Veronese magic to your own holiday celebrations.

3. Beyond the Shopping: Embracing the Festive Spirit

• Live Music and Entertainment: The Christmas markets come alive with festive music, carolers spreading holiday cheer, and performances by local artists. Immerse yourself in the joyful atmosphere and embrace the spirit of the season.

• Ice Skating Rink: Glide across the ice at the Piazza Bra skating rink, offering a perfect winter activity for families and couples. Enjoy the twinkling lights and festive atmosphere while creating lasting Christmas memories.

• Festivities for All Ages: Verona's Christmas markets cater to visitors of all ages. Children will delight in playful carousel rides and traditional Christmas sweets, while adults can sip on mulled wine and soak up the charming atmosphere.

4. Planning Your Christmas Market Adventure

• Opening Hours: The Christmas markets are typically open daily from 10:00 a.m. to 9:30 p.m., with extended hours on weekends. Certain days, like Christmas Eve, may have shorter operating hours, so check in advance.

• Navigating the Crowds: Verona's Christmas markets can get crowded, especially on weekends and evenings.

• Embrace the Cash-Only Culture: While some vendors may accept credit cards, many stalls operate on a cash-only basis. Withdraw euros beforehand to avoid any inconvenience.

• The Perfect Winter Getaway: Verona's Christmas markets offer a delightful escape from the ordinary. Combine your Christmas market exploration with sightseeing, indulging in delicious Veronese cuisine, and exploring the city's historical landmarks.

Chapter 14: Practical Information

Emergency Contacts and Services

1. Important Numbers to Remember:

• National Emergency Number: 112 (This is the equivalent of 911 in many countries and should be used for any life-threatening emergencies, including police, ambulances, or fire brigades.)

• Police: 113 (For non-emergency situations, you can also visit the nearest police station, called "Questura" in Italian.)

• Ambulance: 118 (For medical emergencies requiring immediate medical attention.)

• Fire Brigade: 115 (In case of a fire or other fire-related emergencies.)

2. Additional Resources:

• Verona Emergency Medical Services (Soccorso Verona O.d.v. Ambulanze Verona): +39 349 834 3043

(This private ambulance service operates 24/7 and can be an alternative to calling 118.)

● Borgo Roma Hospital Emergency Room: +39 045 812 4331 (This is the main public hospital in Verona and has a 24/7 emergency room.)

● Verona Tourist Information Center: +39 045 800 0340 (The tourist information center can assist you with various needs, including providing information on nearby pharmacies or hospitals in case of minor emergencies.)

3. Tips for Staying Safe:

● Be Aware of Your Surroundings: As with any tourist destination, it's important to stay vigilant, especially in crowded areas.

● Learn Basic Italian Phrases: Knowing a few key Italian phrases like "aiuto" (help), "polizia" (police), or "ospedale" (hospital) can be helpful in case of an emergency.

● Carry a Photocopy of Your Passport: Keep a photocopy of your passport separate from the original document.

• Purchase Travel Insurance: Consider purchasing travel insurance before your trip. This can provide financial assistance in cases of medical emergencies or unexpected events.

4. Emergency Procedures:

• In Case of a Medical Emergency: If you experience a medical emergency, dial 118 immediately. If possible, try to find someone who speaks English to assist you in explaining the situation to the dispatcher.

• In Case of a Crime: If you are the victim of a crime, dial 113. Do not approach the perpetrator and wait for the police to arrive.

• In Case of a Fire: If you see a fire, dial 115 immediately. Evacuate the area calmly and follow instructions from emergency personnel.

Local Customs and Etiquette

1. Greetings and Interactions:

• A Warm "Buongiorno" or "Buonasera": Always greet shopkeepers, restaurant staff, and anyone you interact with using "Buongiorno" (good morning) until lunchtime and "Buonasera" (good evening) thereafter. A simple "ciao" (hello) is acceptable among friends and younger people.

• The Art of the Handshake: A handshake is the most common form of greeting upon meeting someone for the first time. Maintain eye contact and a firm but gentle handshake. For women, a handshake is perfectly acceptable, but wait for them to initiate it.

• Formal Titles and Respect: Italians value courtesy and respect. Address people with their proper titles (signore for Mr., signora for Mrs./Ms., signorina for young Miss) followed by their last name until a closer relationship develops.

2. Table Manners and Dining Etiquette:

• Slower Pace, Savor the Moment: Unlike some cultures, meals in Verona are a social occasion meant to be savored. Expect a slower pace compared to fast-food dining. Relax, enjoy conversation, and appreciate the food and company.

• "Prego" Please and "Grazie" Thank You: "Prego" can be used both for "please" and "you're welcome." Use "grazie" frequently to express your thanks throughout the meal. Saying "buon appetito" (enjoy your meal) before you start eating is a nice touch.

• Fork and Knife Etiquette: The continental style of dining is customary in Italy. Hold your fork in your left hand and your knife in your right hand throughout the course. Only switch hands when finished with both utensils.

3. Dress Code:

• A Touch of Elegance: Verona leans towards a slightly more dressed-up style compared to some tourist destinations. While casual attire is acceptable for daytime sightseeing, pack clothes that are neat and clean and avoid overly revealing clothing when visiting churches or historical sites. For evenings out, opt for smart casual or semi-formal attire, especially at nicer restaurants.

• Respecting Religious Sites: When visiting churches or religious sites, dress modestly. Cover your shoulders and knees, and avoid wearing hats or sunglasses inside.

4. Tipping in Verona:

A Token of Appreciation: Tipping is not mandatory in Italy, but it's a way to show appreciation for good service. A small tip of 5-10% of the bill rounded up is customary at restaurants. Leave a few euros for good service at bars or cafes. Tipping taxi drivers a small amount is also appreciated.

5. General Social Etiquette:

• Smoking: Smoking is prohibited indoors in most public places, including restaurants and bars. Designated smoking areas are usually available outdoors.

• Public Transportation: Give up your seat on public transportation for the elderly, pregnant women, or people with disabilities.

• Queueing Culture: Italians generally respect queues.

• Siesta Time: Many shops and businesses close for a midday break, typically between 1:00 pm and 4:00 pm. Plan your shopping and errands accordingly.

6. A Few Extra Tips:

• Learn a Few Basic Italian Phrases: Even a few simple Italian phrases like "grazie" (thank you), "prego" (please), or "scusi" (excuse me) go a long way in showing respect and appreciation.

- Embrace the Relaxed Pace: Life in Verona revolves around enjoying the moment. Relax, slow down, and appreciate the city's unique charm.

Cultural Norms

1. Family First:

- The Heart of the Community: Family is the cornerstone of Veronese society. Relationships with extended family are strong, and family gatherings are cherished occasions. Respecting this emphasis on family life goes a long way toward understanding the local culture.

- A Slower Pace of Life: The focus on family often translates to a slower pace of life. Businesses may close for midday breaks (siesta) to prioritize family meals or errands. Embrace this relaxed approach and savor the moment.

2. Food and Social Connections:

- Meals as Social Events: Food is more than just sustenance in Verona; it's a way to connect with loved ones and socialize. Expect longer mealtimes compared to fast-food culture, allowing for conversation and enjoyment of the company.

• Coffee Culture: Coffee is a way of life in Verona. Locals frequent cafes for a quick espresso at the bar or linger over a cappuccino for a leisurely chat with friends or colleagues. Embrace the coffee culture and experience the social buzz of a Veronese cafe.

• The Art of Conversation: Italians are known for their animated conversations and expressive gestures. Don't be surprised by raised voices or lively discussions – it's simply part of their passionate nature.

3. Respecting Traditions:

• Sunday Funday (Mostly): Sundays are typically dedicated to family time and relaxation. Many shops and businesses may be closed, with the exception of tourist hotspots. Plan your shopping and errands accordingly.

• Siestas and Scheduled Breaks: Siesta, the midday break, is a cultural norm in Verona. Many businesses close for a few hours in the afternoon, typically between 1:00 p.m. and 4:00 p.m.. Be prepared for adjusted business hours.

- Dress with Decorum: Verona leans towards a more modest and put-together style compared to some tourist destinations. While casual attire is acceptable for daytime sightseeing, avoid overly revealing clothing, especially when visiting churches or historical sites. Dress modestly when entering religious buildings.

4. Beyond the Basics:

- Celebrating Local Festivals: Immerse yourself in the vibrant culture by attending local festivals throughout the year. From the romantic festivities surrounding Valentine's Day to the lively carnival celebrations, these events offer a glimpse into Veronese traditions.

- Supporting Local Businesses: Verona boasts charming family-run shops and traditional trattorias. By patronizing these local businesses, you support the local economy and get a taste of authentic Veronese products and cuisine.

- A Few Basic Italian Phrases: Learning a few basic Italian phrases like "Buongiorno" (good morning), "Grazie" (thank you), or "Scusi" (excuse me) demonstrates respect for the local language and culture.

Eco-Friendly Practice

1. Sustainable Transportation:

● Exploring by Bike: Verona is a relatively compact city, making it ideal for exploring by bike. The city boasts a well-developed bike-sharing program, Verona Bike, offering a convenient and eco-friendly way to navigate the charming streets.

● Public Transportation: Verona's public transportation system, consisting of buses and trams, is a reliable and affordable way to get around. Opting for public transportation reduces your carbon footprint and allows you to experience the city alongside locals.

● Walking Verona's Streets: Lace up your walking shoes and explore Verona on foot. The historic city center is best experienced at a leisurely pace, allowing you to discover hidden gems and charming alleyways you might miss from a bus or car.

2. Local and Sustainable Food:

● Farmer's Markets: Immerse yourself in the vibrant atmosphere of Verona's farmer's markets. Purchase fresh, seasonal produce directly from local farmers, ensuring you get the best quality ingredients while supporting sustainable farming practices.

● Farm-to-Table Restaurants: Several restaurants in Verona pride themselves on using locally sourced ingredients. These restaurants not only offer delicious meals but also contribute to a more sustainable food system.

● Reduce Food Waste: Italy places a strong emphasis on respecting food. Avoid overordering at restaurants and embrace the concept of "secondi" (seconds) for smaller portions. Leftovers are often wrapped to take home, minimizing food waste.

3. Eco-Conscious Accommodation:

● Eco-Certified Hotels: Verona offers a growing selection of eco-certified hotels that prioritize sustainability practices. These hotels implement measures like energy-efficient lighting, water conservation programs, and waste reduction initiatives.

● Charming B&Bs: Consider staying at a charming bed and breakfast (B&B). B&Bs are often housed in historic buildings and offer a more intimate experience compared to large hotels.

- Support Local Businesses: Opting for locally owned accommodations often translates to smaller establishments with a lower environmental impact. These businesses also contribute to the local economy and community.

4. Beyond the Basics:

- Responsible Souvenirs: When buying souvenirs, seek out locally-made crafts and products. This supports local artisans and reduces the environmental impact associated with mass-produced souvenirs.

- Minimize Waste: Carry a reusable water bottle and shopping bag to reduce your reliance on single-use plastics. Many shops and cafes in Verona are happy to accommodate reusable containers.

- Respect the Environment: Be a responsible tourist by properly disposing of waste and respecting green spaces. Avoid littering and follow designated walking paths in parks and natural areas.

Conclusion

As you close the pages of the "Verona Travel Guide 2024," I hope you are filled with a sense of anticipation and excitement for your journey ahead. Verona, with its blend of historical richness, cultural vibrancy, and picturesque landscapes, offers an unparalleled travel experience. From the echoes of Romeo and Juliet's timeless love story to the grandeur of the Arena di Verona, and from the charming streets of the historic center to the serene banks of the Adige River, every corner of this enchanting city promises discovery and delight.

Recapping your journey through these pages, we've explored Verona's illustrious past and its present-day marvels. We've walked through ancient ruins, admired Renaissance art, and savored the flavors of Veronese cuisine. We've immersed ourselves in local festivals, wandered through lush vineyards, and experienced the warmth and hospitality of the Veronese people. Each chapter has been a step closer to understanding what makes Verona not just a destination but a place that lingers in your heart long after you've left.

 As you set forth on your own adventure, remember that travel is not just about the places you visit but also about the moments you create and the memories you take home. Let Verona's beauty inspire you, let its stories enrich you, and let its spirit captivate you. Embrace the unexpected, seek out the hidden gems, and most importantly, allow yourself to be swept away by the magic that is Verona.

Farewell, dear traveler, and buon viaggio! I hope you have a trip full of wonder, happiness, and life-changing events. Share your stories, spread the enchantment of Verona, and perhaps return someday to uncover even more of its treasures. Until then, keep the spirit of exploration alive and let the world be your guide.

Printed in Great Britain
by Amazon

46818852R00099